THE
CLEANING
NINJA

THE CLEANING NINJA

HOW TO CLEAN YOUR HOME IN 8 MINUTES FLAT AND OTHER CLEVER HOUSEKEEPING TECHNIQUES

COURTENAY HARTFORD
founder of **THE CREEK LINE HOUSE**

PAGE STREET
PUBLISHING CO.

PAGE STREET
PUBLISHING CO.

First published in 2017 by
Page Street Publishing Co.
27 Congress Street, Suite 105
Salem, MA 01970
www.pagestreetpublishing.com

Distributed by Macmillan, sales in Canada by The Canadian Manda Group.

20 19 18 17   1 2 3 4 5

ISBN-13: 978-1-62414-324-3
ISBN-10: 1-62414-324-5

Library of Congress Control Number: 2016943634

Cover and book design by Page Street Publishing Co.

Printed and bound in the United States

Page Street is proud to be a member of 1% for the Planet. Members donate one percent of their sales to one or more of the over 1,500 environmental and sustainability charities across the globe who participate in this program.

To Kennedy, Jack and Chris, who have always helped me to keep my cleaning ninja skills their sharpest.

contents

······························

HOW TO USE
THIS BOOK

This book is all about working smarter,

not harder. It's about getting your home that kind of sparkly clean that you've only dreamed about and doing it with time left over for all the real life-living you want to do in that home. It's meant to be a friend and a source of encouragement when you need a little motivation to get your butt moving, and it's meant to be a solid source of information when you have a housekeeping job that you want to tackle the right way (but so much more quickly than you've done it in the past).

This book is meant to be used, and used, and then used again. It's meant to be open next to you wherever you happen to be working that day, and it's also meant to be an easy book to flip through on the couch when you just want something fun to read. However you want to go about learning how to clean your house a little better, I want to meet you there!

Use this book as a guide and a buddy in your journey out of household chaos. Use it as a reference to look back on for whenever you're ready to tackle a particular project. I like to use the checklists at the end of this book to help me come up with ideas when I'm planning my ninja cleaning time. (That last part will make more sense once you've read the book!) I like to reread a certain chapter about a particular room if that's an area of my home that I want to focus on, both for a burst of motivation and to remind myself of a few clever tips that I may have forgotten about. Yes, I admit it, I did reread my own book—several times, in fact— and my hope is that you will find it so helpful that you will too!

Courtney Hartfield

HOW TO MAKE YOUR HOUSE LOOK CLEAN
in 8 Minutes Flat

We've all been there: it's one of those weeks where everything seems to be blowing up in your face, you're just getting through by the skin of your teeth with all of your household tasks, and suddenly you find out that old friends are going to be in town this afternoon. You can't not invite them over for a little get-together and you don't want to miss out on the chance for some fun times, but your house just isn't presentable. Not the "Oops! Forgot to put away these few toys!" kind of unpresentable, but actually kind of gross. For times like these, you need a plan that works and lets you enjoy your home even amid all of the life-living that's been going on in it. Here it is!

THE PRIORITIES

It's all about focusing on things that your guests (or you) will notice most, that will make your guests feel comfortable in your home, and that make your home seem as clean as possible. Let's be realistic here—we're not going to be passing the white-glove test any time soon, but we can definitely create an environment that feels clean and welcoming to all those who come through our doors. And if you're just taking a few minutes out of your day to regain the feeling of calm and control in your home to make it feel clean and welcoming just for yourself and your family, well, then, that's a great reason to get this quick-clean list done, too!

When it comes to a house that feels cleaner than it really is, your time is most efficiently spent by putting your energy into three things: addressing how your home smells; creating a few shiny, pretty things that will draw the eye; and, of course, removing as much mess and ickiness as possible to make it (hopefully) unnoticeable to the untrained eye.

Since time is of the essence, we'll be focusing on just your most public rooms and the ones your guests will most likely be spending time in. For our purposes today, we'll say that those rooms will be the living room or family room, the kitchen and one main bathroom. You can adapt the concepts that we're going to discuss in this chapter for your home's layout, though. If you need to venture into other rooms in the house to tour your guests around or show them something, well, then, all bets are off. Most people have a few rooms in their house that get a bit crazy sometimes, so don't sweat it too much.

GET IT DONE, MINUTE BY MINUTE

OK. We have eight minutes. We can do this. You can do this. And you're going to. Right now.

We're going to look at our time as eight separate one-minute sessions. First, I'll give you the quick, to-the-point breakdown of how this is all going to happen, then I'll explain each minute in a little more detail afterward.

MINUTE 1: Make the house smell pretty

MINUTE 2: Clear the kitchen counters

MINUTE 3: Clear the kitchen table

MINUTE 4: Clear the junk from the living room

MINUTE 5: Switch out the bathroom hand towel and use it to do a quick wipe-down

MINUTE 6: Quick-scrub the toilet

MINUTE 7: Dust all surfaces

MINUTE 8: Wipe things down

Here's what you'll do for each of these little mini sessions:

MINUTE 1: MAKE THE HOUSE SMELL PRETTY

Fact: A house that smells clean feels clean. Pretty home scents have a way of magically transforming your mess in other people's eyes from "Oh, wow. This house is a total disaster. Just. Wow," to "Oh, look at this happy, wonderful, love-filled, lived-in home!" Any untidiness that you have will suddenly seem like it's just surface clutter that can and will be cleared away in a matter of minutes rather than an indication of complete and utter neglect for basic living standards. The way your house smells will definitely make a difference. If you have time for nothing else, take care of this first!

I like to keep some scented wax melts, scented candles or air spray (from a reputable company that I trust and not some cheap junk that scares me a little to inhale) ready to go for quickness and convenience, but there are so, so, so many ways to make your house smell fresh almost instantly. Check out "Home Scents that Make Sense" on page 105 for lots of other options for next time!

MINUTE 2: CLEAR THE KITCHEN COUNTERS

Let's hit the kitchen first, since that's where we almost always seem to end up when guests are over, either to sit around the table, or to grab some refreshments before sitting down. Since your guests may be consuming food or drinks in this area, we definitely want to make this area feel as sparkly clean as possible!

We're going to clear the counters first and get rid of anything that might give the impression that you have anything less than a perfect record when it comes to keeping up with those kitchen messes. Let's look at what you have on your counters. Maybe some dirty dishes, maybe some papers, maybe some trash—it could be anything really! All kinds of interesting things seem to find a home on our kitchen counters throughout the course of the day, don't they? Let's deal with that trash first. Grab it. Throw it out. Ten seconds. Done. If your kitchen trash can is full, grab a new trash bag and hang it from one of your cabinet knobs. Don't even bother wasting this precious counter minute on changing out your kitchen trash. You can hide the extra trash bag later if you have time, but really, an extra trash bag in your kitchen is so much better than trash all over your counters, so don't worry about it too much.

Next, the dishes. If you have a dishwasher and it's not full, put your dishes in there. If you don't have a dishwasher, or it's totally full, toss (not literally) all of your dishes into your sink, plug it and start running some hot water over them. Squeeze out a little dish soap into the water. Guess what you just did? You totally hid your dirty dishes right in plain sight! They don't read as mess anymore; they just look like you're in the middle of doing the dishes, like any conscientious kitchen owner would be! Pretty clever, right? The scent of that dish soap will also add a little bit of freshness to the room.

What else do you have for me here? Papers? Miscellany? There are a few things you can do to deal with things like this in a quick-clean situation. And I use the term "clean" lightly here. If you have a basket or some kind of organizer on your counter just for this purpose like I do, stick everything in it and call it done. I use a two-tier wire cupcake stand–type of thing—it works great and still looks pretty on the corner of my counter when it's piled with junk. You also have the option of grabbing an extra basket or bin if you have one handy or you can just try to pile everything in a corner semi-neatly. Hey, it's better than nothing! If things are really out of control in the miscellaneous-junk department, you can also just grab everything and throw it into a bedroom or a closet or the shower and just shut the door or pull the curtain. It's not ideal, but it definitely works in a pinch!

MINUTE 3: CLEAR THE KITCHEN TABLE

A clear kitchen table is both a great place to sit down with your guests with a cup of tea and some snacks and something that instantly makes your whole room look cleaner. You've heard how making your bed can suddenly make your bedroom appear 80 percent cleaner, and it's really pretty much the same thing with your kitchen table.

The same concepts that you used with your counters apply here, so get to it! Trash that trash, toss those dishes in the dishwasher or sink, and add to the pile you created when you were clearing your miscellaneous counter junk. Easy. Done.

 ## MINUTE 4: CLEAR THE JUNK FROM THE LIVING ROOM

Living rooms are generally made to be pretty, welcoming spaces, so it doesn't take much to make everything seem right in this room. This is probably my favorite room in the house to transform with the one-minute tidy-up because of what a difference only a few seconds of stuff-clearing can make in here. What kind of junk have you got for me here? Toys, clothing, blankets, dishes? Start with any dirty dishes first, set those together near the doorway that takes you toward your kitchen and then move on to everything else. For all the other objects in the room, start with the largest ones first and put away or hide everything that you can. You'll get better at this the more times you work this quick-clean plan, but for now, every little bit helps! You can always toss a blanket over the back of your couch or straighten a cushion later when you walk into this room with your guests.

Next, we'll be in the bathroom, so if you're headed back in the direction of the kitchen on your way there, bring your dishes with you. If not, leave them and come back for them after you're done everything else. You can just toss them into your sink or dishwasher when you have the chance.

MINUTE 5: SWITCH OUT THE BATHROOM HAND TOWEL AND USE IT TO DO A QUICK WIPE-DOWN

Using a wet hand towel to dry your hands after using the bathroom in someone else's house is probably one of the ickiest things out there, so let's make sure that doesn't happen to your guests today. Grab the old hand towel, wipe out your sink and whatever surrounding areas you can get to quickly and put out a fresh hand towel. If you don't have any clean hand towels ready to go, just take a full-size towel and neatly fold it on the counter or lay it over the edge of the sink.

MINUTE 6: QUICK-SCRUB THE TOILET

Yes. Do this. You'll be so glad you did. Any type of soap will do. Just squirt a little in the toilet bowl, swish the brush around to remove any stains and then finish up by wiping the top of the toilet tank, the seat and the rim of the bowl with a bit of toilet paper, working from the cleanest area to the dirtiest. Toss it in the toilet bowl, flush and you're done! Now you have a bathroom that's thoroughly unterrifying for your guests to use! There may still be bath toys all over the room, but at least everything that will be physically touched is clean and safe.

MINUTE 7: DUST ALL SURFACES

It's amazing how removing a little dust can brighten up a space! Move through your kitchen and living room with a feather duster if you have one (or a soft, dry cloth if you don't). For quick dusting, you want to focus on anything in a dark color first, because those are the places that are most likely to show dust. Look at things like dark wood furniture, blank TVs and any light fixtures with dark metal parts on them. You'll be thrilled with what a difference this minute will make overall!

 ## MINUTE 8: WIPE THINGS DOWN

Grab three or four soft cloths and quickly wet them under the tap, which will be much quicker than trying to spray each individual surface down as you go. Start in the kitchen and work your way into the living room, focusing on wiping any surface that your guests will physically touch, like the kitchen table and chairs or the coffee table, to remove any stickiness. Once everything is good there, move on to your favorite pretty, shiny objects. A few shiny things will draw the eye and really distract from any small bits of untidiness that you have left in these rooms, so wipe down your favorite shiny wood furniture, pretty wall clocks, fancy lamps and other favorite decorative objects. Each time a cloth is used on a particularly sticky surface (or just one that happened to still have quite a bit of dust on it), switch out to a new cloth. This will save you from going over the same surface multiple times.

So that's your eight minutes! If you happened to really only have exactly eight minutes to work with, congratulate yourself on what a huge difference you've made in your home in such a short amount of time and enjoy it! If you still have time to spare, use it! Tidy up a few more things here and there, make yourself look a little more presentable or make yourself a quick snack. You've earned it!

HERE ARE A FEW *bonus* THINGS YOU CAN DO TO MAKE A BIG DIFFERENCE IF YOU STILL HAVE A FEW EXTRA MOMENTS TO WORK WITH:

START A JOB.

In-progress jobs are just fine to have out in plain sight. Tell your guests that they just caught you right in the middle of doing your normal cleaning. They also make it look like you were just about to get to all those other little things that still need to be done, too!

RUN SOME MACHINES.

If your dishwasher and washing machine aren't too loud and obnoxious-sounding, get them started. The sounds of cleaning whirring away in the background really help to clear away any sense of a house being neglected for a little too long.

TURN ON SOME MORE LIGHTS.

Things that are clean are often called "bright and shiny." You've already taken care of the "shiny" part, so add some brightness to make things sparkle!

SETTING UP AN EFFICIENT *Cleaning Pantry*

Your cleaning-supply area should be among the most organized areas in your home if you're looking to speed up and improve your cleaning game. This is command central for keeping your home clean and tidy (*and* doing it as quickly as possible), so being able to find everything and having everything you need right there will go a long way toward making your life easier and, ultimately, saving you tons of time.

FIND A SPACE

You'll want to set up your cleaning pantry in an area that's easily accessible and centrally located in your home. Being able to grab what you need right when you need it is a key to success in keeping your home as sparkly clean as you'd like it to be. Basic cleaners and cloths should be easy to grab, right at eye-level, with brushes and dusters just below or above. You'll need a tall space to keep brooms and mops and potentially a bit of extra space for your vacuum cleaner, depending on the model. If this all sounds like a lot to keep in one closet or cupboard in your home, you can definitely store things in several different areas, just make sure that you're making life simple for yourself by keeping things easily accessible and storing items that will be used together in the same spot. If you find yourself bending over a lot or getting up on a chair to grab something that you use every day, then you should definitely try to figure out a new storage spot, as these actions can get just plain annoying over time and will really end up discouraging you from keeping up with your cleaning jobs in the long run.

GETTING THE TOOLS

There are so many cleaning tools and gadgets available these days at nearly every supermarket or big-box store. Some of them are great, and some aren't worth the cheap plastic that they're made from. Of course, if you're like most people, you probably already know this because you've probably tried quite a few of those cleaning doodads and thingamajigs over the years.

ESSENTIAL CLEANING TOOLS AND SUPPLIES

You don't need to spend a lot of money on your cleaning tools overall. For the most part, basics will do the job quite nicely. But for some things, like with a feather duster or your vacuum cleaner, it pays to get the best that you can afford to really see those speedy and shiny results that you've been looking for. This is a list of tried-and-true tools and supplies that will really work and get you set up to clean your home quickly, easily and with as little annoyance as possible:

- Soft cotton cloths, such as white terry towels or cheap washcloths

- Microfiber cloths

- Basic large bath towels (reserved only for cleaning)

- Basic corn broom

- Small, handheld dust brush

- Dust pan

- Basic cotton mop

- Dust mop

- Lightweight vacuum cleaner

- Wet/dry vacuum cleaner, such as the Shop-Vac brand

(continued)

- Bucket

- Scrub brush with stiff bristles

- Steel wool

- Abrasive scouring pads

- Scratch-free scouring pads

- Large sponges

- Box of disposable rubber or latex gloves

- Small detail brush (or a toothbrush)

- Good-quality feather duster

- Squeegee

- Plastic scraper

- Paper towels

- Old newspapers

CLEANING SOLUTIONS AND POTIONS

For convenience, it's nice to have a store-bought cleaner or two in a spray bottle, ready to go when you have a quick cleaning job to do. It's really not necessary at all, though, to go out and buy the entire cleaning aisle at your grocery store. For the most part, you can do a really great, effective job of cleaning your whole home if you have your cleaning pantry stocked with just a few basic ingredients. Using these cleaners along with the right tools and, of course, a few tricks and techniques up your sleeve, will get you far better results than most "miracle" cleaners from the store. There are a few exceptions to the rule that are nice to have for especially difficult cleaning scenarios and I've noted those on the next page:

- Vinegar

- Lemon juice

- Isopropyl rubbing alcohol

- Baking soda

- Cheap olive oil reserved just for cleaning

- Borax

- Basic dish soap

- Natural wax- or oil-based furniture polish

- Basic all-purpose cleaner in a spray bottle for quick cleanups

- Glass cleaner or a homemade alternative

- Heavy-duty laundry stain remover for laundry, upholstery and carpet stain emergencies

- Heavy-duty concentrated cleaner for really dirty floors and outdoor jobs

- Lime and rust stain remover for hard-water deposits

These are the cleaners that are nice to keep in your main cleaning pantry, and this list doesn't include things like laundry soap, fabric softener and dishwasher soap that you'll need to keep in those specific areas of the house.

With these few basic items at the ready, you'll be all set for some housekeeping magic! Your home is your oyster! Let's get to it.

THE
EVERYDAY
LIST: TRICKS
TO MAKE
Your Life Easier

There are things around the house that you just have to do every day to keep things running smoothly for your family. Everyone's daily routine is a little different of course, but you should be able to find more than a few tips in here that will apply to your own "everyday list." If you have a few tricks up your sleeve that are able to help you out every day with these little tasks, the payoff in terms of the amount of time that you'll save in the long run will be huge!

TIP ONE

Use your hand towel to wipe out your bathroom sink every day, and then replace it with a new one. The larger surface area (compared to smaller rags) and super-absorbent material will make getting your sink sparkly clean take about 3.8 seconds and—bonus!—you'll suddenly be one of those people who always has a fresh hand towel out!

TIP TWO

Go over all the mirrors and glass surfaces in your home quickly with a feather duster every few days to go much longer between cleaning and polishing them with a cloth and glass cleaner. Honestly, 98.4% of the "mess" that you see on these surfaces is just dust and pet fur that has settled there, not legitimate streaks and fingerprints. OK, that's a totally made-up stat, but this tip really does make all the difference!

TIP THREE

Furniture polish isn't just for furniture! Once in a while, use furniture polish as an "everyday wipe-up" spray on things like appliances, trim, tabletops or anywhere that you see gunk, dust and fingerprints building up on a regular basis. The polish helps keep these messes from appearing on surfaces for a lot longer, and makes that gunk we spoke about earlier slide right off when it's time for you to wipe those surfaces clean again in the future.

TIP FOUR

Here's a note for pet lovers: Always "top-dress" your freshly scooped cat litter with a little sprinkling of baking soda at least a few times a week. Even if you use a cat litter with baking soda in it, you'll be amazed at how much longer your litter will stay odorless and how much easier it will be to scoop every day. It's like having a nonstick litter box!

TIP FIVE

Keep spills and leaks from causing a mess in the bottom of your kitchen garbage can by lining it with a fresh sheet or two of old newspaper each time you change out the bag. Not only will you never have to rinse out a sticky garbage can again, but the newspaper will actually help to absorb offensive odors as well!

TIP SIX

Don't underestimate the power of soap and water. Put a wet, soapy cloth in your hand once a day and be amazed at all the things that just suddenly seem to clean themselves. It only takes a minute or two each day to wipe up a few drips and spills here and there, but you'll love what a difference a soapy cloth will make in a room when you stand back and admire your work! Filling your sink with hot soapy water as part of the process will keep it clean and flush out your drains when you're done. I know, I know. It sounds so simple and old-fashioned that plain ol' soap and water can't possibly be of any help in a modern home with all the latest cleaning machines and new-age cleaning products available on the market, but just you wait! I was just as surprised as you will be when I finally broke down and gave in to this old-fashioned "trick"—if you can call it that.

TIP SEVEN

Keep up with the easy stuff like laundry and dishes every day, and they *really will* start to feel like the easy stuff! Dirty laundry, crusty dishes and appliances that sit without running for days on end will really start to affect the overall freshness of your home, both in appearance and in smell! Spending a moment or two each day just to keep things moving in these areas of your home will make you feel like you're really starting to get the hang of this housekeeping thing!

TIP EIGHT

Invest in a small collection of baskets that you love in different shapes and sizes and then watch their magical powers transform your home. A great-looking basket can tidy a room *and* decorate it in a matter of seconds. Try to get baskets that will look good in any room in your home so you can switch them out and use them for different purposes at different times of the year. A large basket can be a quick solution to hold extra toys in the living room at Christmastime, and then it can be a place to put all of those extra flips flops, skipping ropes and soccer balls by the door in the summer. Use them liberally all over the house to make your home look stylish and put together in a flash. Empty them out and put everything away when you notice you aren't using the contents on a regular basis anymore or when seasons change.

TIP NINE

Use so, so many cloths. No matter what job you're working on. If it involves wiping, always triple the amount of cloths that your common sense would tell you is appropriate for the task. We always assume it's best to rinse out the same cloth and use it again, but for most jobs, it's much quicker and more effective to just use a new cloth once the first one is full of mess and then toss them all into the wash. When you start to actually pay attention, you'll be surprised by how much time you waste trying to pick up that same little bit of dust or pet fur on a surface, redepositing it again by accident, and then trying to pick it up with a fresh spot on the cloth, only to find that the fresh spot already has more dust on it. Once you start providing yourself with an adequate amount of clean cloths for a job, you'll look back on the little "picking it up and putting it back down" game that you used to play with grime and a single measly cloth and it will almost be comical that you ever put yourself through that just to save a few square inches of space in your washing machine.

And it's as easy as that! A few little changes to the way you think about your daily cleanup can make a big difference!

THE
SINGLE MOST
IMPORTANT
HABIT THAT
YOU NEED TO
Start Doing Right Away

You know what I'm going to say. You need to make your bed. Yes, you do. Shush. Just do it. You've probably heard this before, but have you really ever stopped to think about *why* this one habit is so important and can have such a positive effect on your whole home? I know that you've probably spent a lot of time coming up with some really smart-sounding ideas for why *not* to make the bed in the morning, so let me just give you some more things to think about while you're being all clever and thoughtful. Then give the bed-making a try for a while. Just to see. Even just to prove the point that you were right all along. I promise you're going to love the way it makes your home look and makes *you* feel. And if not, you can have full "I told you so" bragging rights.

IT'S *SO* EASY

Again, this is one that you're just going to have to trust me on. Take a leap of faith! Not a very big leap, but maybe still a leap nonetheless. It will take about twenty-seven seconds for you to see how right I am about this. There's really nothing to it! Just flop some pillows on there, pull up the covers, smooth them out and you're done!

IT LOOKS NICE

This really goes without saying, but it gives you one more thing to admire and appreciate in your home as you walk in and out of your room throughout the day. You want your home to look nice and clean, and making your bed is one of the quickest ways to achieve that. It only makes sense for a smart, logical person like you to make your bed every day, right?

IT CAN HELP WITH ALLERGIES

If you're someone who suffers from allergies, then this reason may be especially important for you. Keeping your bed covered up keeps dust and allergens from accumulating between the sheets and on your pillow throughout the day and gives you a peaceful place where you can breathe easily all night long.

IT'S THE THIRTY-SECOND ROOM MAKEOVER

Nothing takes a messy room from looking completely chaotic to mostly tidy faster than sticking a freshly made bed right in the middle of it. If you struggle with a cluttered bedroom, making the bed every day will give you a big jump-start on your tidy-up mission!

IT GIVES YOU A SMALL SENSE OF ACCOMPLISHMENT TO START THE DAY

You know that feeling where you're on a roll and being so productive and you just feel like you could take on the world? Those kind of days always start with one accomplishment that makes you feel so good about yourself and about getting stuff done that you just can't seem to stop yourself from accomplishing task after task from your to-do list. Why not have that kind of day every day, automatically, by creating a beautiful, clean space first thing when you wake up?

IT'S A REWARD AT THE END OF THE DAY

There's just something so satisfying about crawling into a nicely made bed at the end of the day. It's the perfect way to end a productive day that you can be proud of or to comfort yourself and remind yourself that all is still right in the world on those days when you're just *dog tired*. Even if you've had a rough day, being able to get into a freshly made bed will put you in a positive mindset and end your day on a happy and hopeful note.

IT WILL MAKE YOU FEEL LIKE A MASTER OF DOMESTICITY

There's nothing better than having people drop by your house unexpectedly and being able to open up your doors to them without having to give the condition of your home a second thought. It's pretty easy to make one or two main rooms look presentable, but a lot of people feel anxiety over a bedroom door left open that guests can happen to look into on their way down the hall to use the bathroom. It feels amazing to know that they'll see that your bed is made, will almost definitely notice, and will most certainly be impressed at what a good job you do of keeping your home tidy—even when people arrive without notice. You might not want to admit it, but just try to *not* feel proud of yourself the first time that you find yourself in that situation!

IT TELLS YOU SOMETHING ABOUT YOURSELF

You already know what kind of people are the diligent bed-makers of the world. They're the people with integrity, the people with vision, the people with stick-to-itiveness, the leaders, the initiative takers and the goal accomplishers. They're those successful people with the kind of self-discipline that you can't help but admire. There's a reason that many, many wise and successful people swear by starting their day with making their bed, and that's because it really is a game-changer in their homes and in their lives. Every time you make your bed or see that you've made your bed earlier in the day, you're reminding yourself that you're one of those people, too.

SNEAKY TRICKS FOR MAKING A BED
super quickly

IGNORE YOUR SLEEPING PILLOWS

Don't try to fluff them or rearrange them too much or make them look presentable at all. You and I both know that's just a waste of your precious time!

COVER UP WITH EXTRA BASIC PILLOWS

Purchase two or three extra regular pillows, just enough to go all the way across the top of your bed and cover your sleeping pillows. Don't use these pillows for sleep at all, but instead keep them just for providing a nice, full, structured look to your bed and for hiding those crunched-up pillows that you sleep on every night!

USE ONE OR TWO ACCENT PILLOWS THAT GO IN THE SAME PLACE EVERY DAY

Any more than one or two accent pillows on your bed will lead you to fuss over their placement and will probably just make you feel frustrated in your early-morning, fuzzy-brain state. Instead, choose a couple of pillows that you like, decide where you're going to put them, and then do it exactly the same way every day. It's pillow autopilot!

(continued)

SNEAKY TRICKS FOR MAKING A BED
super quickly (CONTINUED)

GO SYMMETRICAL

For a really tidy, finished look, keep your whole bed scheme symmetrical. It's the ultimate cleaned-up look and it requires zero thought first thing in the morning.

A TEXTURED QUILT OR DUVET COVER WON'T SHOW WRINKLES

A quilt with a pattern stitched into it or a duvet cover with a lot of texture will resist wrinkles and will look stylish and freshly laundered day after day, whereas a flat duvet cover or comforter is almost impossible to get wrinkle-free without spending hours with an iron and will look a little messy no matter what you do.

SKIP THE EXTRA FOLDED BLANKET AND THE TOSSED-JUST-SO THROW

If you're in the habit of folding an extra decorative blanket at the foot of your bed or tossing a throw "just so" on one corner, you can save a lot of time and actually make your bed look more finished by removing that from your routine. No blanket at all looks so much tidier than a haphazardly folded or awkwardly tossed one any day.

DO IT EVERY DAY

The more bed-making days that you have under your belt, the better (and faster) you'll get at it! You'll start to put the pillows down in the same spot every night and you'll be able to grab them in a flash and pop them back onto your bed exactly right without even thinking about it. You'll also know which corner of the sheets you always seem to pull out in your sleep and which way to tug the covers to get them to line up like a pro. A smart (and busy) person like you can't help but get better and better at something as time goes on, and I can't wait to see where your soon-to-be amazing bed-making skills are going to take you now that you've learned how to start your days off right!

THE CLEANEST
KITCHEN
on the Block

Kitchens are definitely some of the dirtiest, grimiest, greasiest places in our homes. We all probably spend a lot of our cleaning time and energy trying to keep things in check in there, but the good news is that conquering the kitchen mess once and for all is not only some of the most challenging work you'll do around the house, it can also be the most rewarding. If you want that "I've been scrubbing all day" look to your kitchen without that "I've been scrubbing all day" experience, you're in luck! Here are some of the best ways to get the most out of your cleaning time in the kitchen:

- If the idea of wiping down every single one of your sticky kitchen cabinets seems less than appealing to you, try this method! Make a solution of one-half warm soapy water and one-half white vinegar in a bucket and grab yourself a nice stack of soft cloths. First, wipe down a section of three or four cabinets with a cloth heavily soaked in the solution, wait thirty seconds or so, then go back over with a cloth that's only slightly damp and pick up all the excess water. Let the solution do the work for you and keep your motions relaxed. No scrubbing needed *or* allowed here! This method is easier on your cabinets' finish in the long run and keeps you from dreading having to work your hands to the bone cleaning bits of jam and gunk off of every single cupboard door.

- For a smelly garbage disposal, pour ½ cup (103 g) of baking soda and 1 cup (240 ml) of vinegar down your disposal drain, then toss in a handful of frozen lemons and limes. Turn it on and let it clean itself! Not only will it smell so much fresher, but the ice from the lemons and limes will help scrape any food residue out of your disposal *and* the ice will sharpen the blades!

- For grout on a kitchen backsplash that may have acquired a bit of greasy buildup, make a paste of baking soda and water and scrub your grout lines in the affected area with an old toothbrush.

- The best thing for cleaning a white porcelain sink easily and quickly can be found right in your kitchen! Just mix up a paste of baking soda and dish soap using about ¼ cup (52 g) of baking soda and enough basic dish soap to make a nice runny paste in a little dish. Take a soft cloth and gently polish your entire sink, then rinse off for a shine like you haven't seen since it was brand new! If you've been trying to get stains out of your sink by soaking it in harsh chemicals for hours at a time only to be disappointed, you'll be pleasantly surprised at how well this simple solution works!

- A dull and darkened stainless steel sink can be brought back to life by filling it up with a solution of half water and half white vinegar. Leave it to sit for an hour or so, then use a medium-bristled brush to scrub down the entire surface as well as around the drain. If you have an old sink full of scratches and dings, use a scouring pad in a circular motion to gently buff all the scratches away.

- If your dishwasher isn't quite performing like it used to, try running a quick cleaning cycle to help your dishes sparkle and keep everything smelling fresh and clean. Place a dishwasher-safe cup full of white vinegar on the top rack and run a full cycle. Next, sprinkle a cup of baking soda in the bottom of your dishwasher and run it through a full cycle again. Repeat these steps once per month to keep your dishwasher healthy and happy!

- You can make your own "rinse aid" for the dishwasher to help dishes get squeaky clean and prevent cloudiness by placing a cup full of vinegar on the top rack of the dishwasher during each wash cycle. Never put vinegar straight into the rinse aid compartment though because vinegar just sitting in there for days or weeks at a time can damage some of the internal workings of your machine.

- One little trick that saves more time than you'd think: always load your dishwasher with similar items together. Put all the forks in the same section of the cutlery rack, all the mugs together, all the glasses, all the plates and so on. It seems silly, but you really do waste a lot of energy going back and forth to different cupboards over and over again while you're unloading.

- If you have blackened bits of food at the bottom of your favorite pot or pan, try soaking the pots overnight in water with a dryer sheet. Either submerge the whole thing in a sink of water with the dryer sheet or just fill up the pot and toss the dryer sheet right in. Leave it to sit for a few hours or overnight and everything will just wipe right off!

- Copper-bottomed pots that have lost their shine can be easily restored by taking a half of a lemon, dipping it into salt and then using that as a scrubber directly on the copper. Unlike some other solutions, this one works instantly!

- If your favorite baking sheets have seen better days, you can restore them by using a paste of hydrogen peroxide and baking soda to clean them. Allow the paste to sit on your baking sheets overnight if they're very heavily soiled.

- To keep new baking sheets clean and looking their best, line them with parchment paper or aluminum foil each time you use them, especially if you're cooking with fats or oils.

- Clean cloudy dishes in a half-and-half solution of vinegar and water. For dishes that already have a cloudy buildup from too many cycles through the dishwasher, soak them in a sink filled with a half-and-half vinegar and water solution for a few hours and then wipe them clean with a damp cloth. The vinegar will wash all of the cloudy mineral deposits right away!

- A good supply of scouring pads and no-scratch scouring pads can outdo any harsh chemical or "non-harsh-chemical" cleaning solution on a lot of your toughest jobs. Sometimes it's best to just save yourself the time and frustration and get scrubbing!

- Another great solution for cooked-on messes: if your last culinary adventure left you with food burned on to the bottom of your favorite frying pan, fill it about halfway with water, add in a few tablespoons of lemon juice and put the pan on the stove. "Cook" the water and lemon juice until it comes to a low boil, then take a plastic spoon or spatula and gently scrape the blackened food bits. They'll come off easily, cleanly and instantly!

- Microwave dish sponges on high for two minutes to kill germs. This will make your sponges last longer and make them clean more effectively!

- Clean your blender by adding warm water and a few drops of dish soap, then turn it on low for a few minutes. Rinse it out and you're ready to go for next time!

- Restore shine and brightness to cutlery by soaking it in a half-and-half solution of water and vinegar. Leave them to sit for about half an hour and then wipe them clean with a damp cloth; your cutlery will look like new!

- Rest bottles of honey, vanilla, cooking oils, vinegars and other culprits of leakiness on cupcake liners to keep cabinet shelves clean. Pull the liners out and replace them when they start to get dirty or sticky to prevent pests in your kitchen.

- A glass cooktop that's had one too many pots boil over on it can be a real mess and a hassle to get clean. If this sounds like a familiar situation in your house, all you need is some baking soda and some damp rags. Sprinkle the baking soda over the entire cooktop, then layer the damp rags right over the top of the baking soda. Let this sit for thirty minutes or so, then use the rags to wipe everything away. If anything remains on your cooktop at that point, simply use the rags to scrub the baking soda into those areas and remove whatever's left!

- For your dirtiest, grimiest, cakiest stove grates, all you need is ½ cup (120 ml) of ammonia and a heavy plastic bag. You can use either large size zip-top bags to do each grate individually or one large garbage bag to do all your grates at once. Place the grates in the bag, add the ammonia and let them sit overnight outside. In the morning, remove the grates and you'll be able to wipe them clean easily.

- A pumice stone is a great way to clean the baked on stuff out of your oven without having to use any harsh chemicals. The pumice stone will make quick work of the charred spills and splatters, but it's soft enough that it won't scratch the inside of your oven. (Definitely use a clean one and not the one out of the shower that you use to make your feet look cute in sandals!)

- Vent hoods should be cleaned regularly to keep them working at peak performance. Just use a large pot of boiling water, toss in about ½ cup (103 g) of baking soda and then soak each vent hood filter in the pot and watch the magic happen! You may need to do one side of each filter at a time if your filters are too big to fit in your pot.

LIGHTNING-
FAST LAUNDRY

Laundry is probably the number one
most complained about household chore in the entire universe. It seems like we all hear someone cracking a joke about their giant pile of laundry almost every day. The amazing thing is, though, that laundry is really the easiest thing to get a handle on in most homes with a few very simple changes to your laundry routine. Add in a few sneaky tricks to make your washing time more effective and speedier, and you'll wonder how you ever even gave your laundry pile a second thought!

MAKING LAUNDRY TIME QUICKER

Who doesn't wish that laundry time could pass a little more quickly? Even those of us that kind of not-so-secretly enjoy doing the laundry would still get all the satisfaction and enjoyment out of the task if it felt like it was done in the blink of an eye, really. Then we could just have time to do *more* laundry! Yay! OK, now I'm just kidding, mostly . . .

I'd better just go ahead and jump right into these time-saving tips before you start to think I've completely lost my marbles. Whether you truly enjoy laundry or you totally dread it, you'll appreciate these tricks that I've picked up along the way to help you love your laundry just a little more:

- Did you know that most laundry items no longer need to be sorted? I really see sorting laundry as from the dark ages and mostly a waste of time. Sure, if I have a load of really dirty white soccer uniforms that need some extra love and maybe a brightening treatment, I'll wash those separately, but that's really more of a special circumstance and definitely not an everyday thing. Dye technologies and colorfastness have improved to the point where you really can just toss everything from your laundry basket straight into the wash together! So free yourself from the shackles of separating your laundry for hours!

- Speaking of separating laundry, there is *one* exception! Have a separate laundry basket where you keep clothes with stains that you know will need a bit of extra work before going into the laundry. This saves you from spending precious minutes searching through all those dirty clothes to find that one pair of pants with the grass stains *and* it keeps you from forgetting to treat the stains at all and then setting them permanently in the dryer, yet again.

- Try to do at least one load of laundry a day (or even just one *part* of a load of laundry a day). It could be that you run the washing machine and the dryer in one day, fold the next and put everything away on the third day. Use whatever system of laundry steps that works for you. Staying on top of your laundry really makes it easier to get a quick start without giant piles everywhere slowing you down or making you feel overwhelmed.

- Don't overclean your clothes. For most regular laundry, the "quick wash" setting really is enough and it could save you thirty to forty minutes on each load! That really adds up! Along those same lines, don't clean your clothes if they're not dirty. A sweater worn over a T-shirt for an hour running errands in town will usually only need to be hung up and aired out for a bit rather than completely washed and dried. Your clothes will definitely look newer for longer, too, so it really makes sense to only wash things that actually need washing. In fact, some people swear that you should never wash blue jeans at all and just store them in the freezer to kill off any smelly bacteria. Well, OK, yeah, that one kind of grosses me out a little too . . . but you get the idea.

- Stay organized. Have everything you might need within arm's reach in your laundry room. You'll want to have a small trash can for dryer lint, a basket or bin for single socks, a basket for separating stained items that need to be pretreated like I mentioned earlier, and a container or tray for mystery items you find in pockets or bumping around in the dryer. No matter how many times I check pockets, I always seem to end up with a tractor key floating around in the dryer, so it's good to have a place where we always know we can find it when we need it again!

- Always use the cool-temperature, automatic-dry function instead of high heat in your dryer. It will keep your clothes newer-looking for longer and is usually faster overall than just running every dryer load through for the same amount of time. The automatic feature will save you from having to put certain items back in the dryer that are still too wet while others are ready to be folded and put away.

- You can also save time in the dryer by adding in one large dry towel to each load to help absorb extra moisture, cutting down on your overall drying time!

- Line the top of your ironing board with tin foil to create a reflective surface that cuts ironing time in half by heating up the back side of your fabric as well!

MAKING LAUNDRY TIME MORE EFFECTIVE

What's the point of even doing the laundry if it doesn't actually get things *clean*, right? Here are some of my favorite tips for making sure you really know what you're doing when it comes to laundry issues of all sorts:

- Only use warm or cool water when pretreating stains. Water that's either too cold or too hot can set some stains permanently.

- Refresh your towels every few months to restore their absorption and get rid of any musty smells by first washing them in a load using only a ½ cup (103 g) of baking soda sprinkled inside the machine before loading, then wash them again, this time adding in about ½ cup (120 ml) of vinegar instead of detergent. Finish up by drying them without dryer sheets and your towels will be at least as good as new, but probably even better!

- Keep a dry-erase marker in your laundry room so you can make notes to yourself right on the top of your dryer or your dryer door to remind yourself of items that need to be air dried only.

- Putting 1 teaspoon (5 g) of table salt in a load of laundry will help keep colors brighter and will help prevent color bleeding in those few items that may still be prone to it.

- Make your own laundry scent booster to keep clothes smelling fresh for longer by combining 3 cups (618 g) of baking soda, 3 cups (724 g) of Epsom salts, 30 drops of orange essential oil and 30 drops of lavender essential oil. Use about ¼ cup (52 g) of the mixture per load, directly in your washing machine tub on top of your laundry.

- Make your own super-whitening presoak by mixing 1 cup (240 ml) of hydrogen peroxide, ¼ cup (60 ml) of lemon juice and 2 cups (475 ml) of water. Store it in a glass jar and pour it over any whites that need an extra boost before wash time, or soak them overnight for really serious dinginess issues. It works on clothing, pillows, bedding and towels, and the lemon juice gives them an amazing fresh scent!

- Let the sun do the heavy lifting when it comes to stain removal. We all know that the sun has a bleaching effect on furniture, rugs and prints that are positioned near a bright window, so why not put it to work? If you have a really tough stain that won't seem to come out, try leaving it outside to dry in the sun on a hot day. This is also a great idea after doing a brightening treatment on a load of whites!

- Clean your washing machine regularly to avoid funky-smelling loads of laundry that end up needing to be rewashed (or that make you walk around wondering what that weird smell is all day until you finally realize that it's your sweater). All you need to do is run a hot-water or whites cycle in your machine while it's empty and add in 2 cups (480 ml) of vinegar directly into the tub of your machine. Run an additional hot cycle without any detergent or vinegar to rinse everything out.

- To get rid of wrinkles in clothes that may have sat unfolded a little too long, make your own wrinkle-releasing spray by adding ¼ cup (60 ml) of liquid fabric softener and ¼ cup (60 ml) of vinegar to an empty spray bottle and then filling it to the top with water. Shake, shake, shake and then you're ready to be wrinkle-free!

THE STAIN
TRAUMA
Center

Accidents happen, and when they do, these tools and techniques should be your go-to recovery methods.

Dab all of these stain fighters directly onto the stain unless an alternative method is mentioned:

- **BALL-POINT INK:** Hairspray + water (apply the hairspray to the stain, let it sit for a few minutes, then rinse it out with warm water)

- **BARBECUE SAUCE:** Cool water + vinegar + dish soap

- **BEET:** Cool water + hydrogen peroxide + baking soda

- **BERRIES:** Cold water + vinegar or warm water + hydrogen peroxide + baking soda (pour the warm water through the stain into a bowl, then use a paste of hydrogen peroxide and baking soda to treat the stain directly)

(continued)

- **BLOOD OR OTHER BODILY FLUIDS:** Salt + cool water or hydrogen peroxide (place 1 tablespoon [15 g] of salt in a bowl of water and leave it to soak overnight)

- **CANDLE WAX:** Iron + paper towels (layer the paper towels over the wax and iron on top to melt the wax into the paper towel)

- **CHARCOAL OR ASH:** cool water + dish soap

- **CHOCOLATE:** Warm water + dish soap (rinse the stain from the reverse side, then use dish soap)

- **COFFEE:** Water + vinegar

- **CRAYON:** Baking soda + dry cloth (sprinkle the stain with baking soda and then rub with a cloth)

- **DEODORANT:** Baking soda + hydrogen peroxide + water

- **GLUE:** Cool water + hydrogen peroxide + baking soda (mix all three ingredients together and soak the stain in this solution until it's softened enough to be removed or rinsed away)

- **GRASS:** Vinegar + dish soap + cool water (saturate the stain with vinegar, then soak it in a bowl of cool water and dish soap)

- **GREASE OR OIL:** Baking soda + dish soap, chalk or rubbing alcohol

- **GUM:** Ice (rub the gum with an ice cube until it's frozen and hard enough to remove from the fabric)

- **HAIR DYE:** Hairspray + warm water + laundry detergent (soak the stain in hairspray first and let it sit for thirty minutes, then wash by hand with detergent and warm water)

- **MAKEUP (EYE MAKEUP):** Oil-free makeup remover + dish soap

- **MAKEUP (FOUNDATION):** Shaving cream + clean cloth (apply the shaving cream directly to the stain and allow it to sit for a few minutes, then gently lift the makeup pigment out of the fabric using a dry cloth)

- **MAKEUP (LIPSTICK):** Hairspray + cool water

- **MARKER:** Rubbing alcohol + paper towel (apply the rubbing alcohol directly to the stain, then use a paper towel to gently soak up the marker pigment; keep switching to a clean area of the paper towel as it becomes marked with pigment)

- **MEAT AND GRAVY:** Dish soap + warm water + baking soda

- **MUD OR DIRT:** Dish soap + warm water

- **MUSTARD:** Cool water + hydrogen peroxide + baking soda + dish soap (rinse the stain first in the cool water, then make a paste of the remaining three ingredients to treat the stain directly)

- **NAIL POLISH:** Non-acetone nail polish remover

- **PAINT:** Hairspray + stiff-bristled brush (apply the hairspray to the stain, allow it to sit for a few minutes, then gently loosen the paint using a stiff-bristled brush)

- **RED WINE OR GRAPE JUICE:** White wine or hydrogen peroxide

- **RUST:** Cream of tartar + hydrogen peroxide (mix the two ingredients to form a paste and apply it directly to the stain)

- **SOFT DRINKS:** Dish soap + vinegar

- **SWEAT STAINS:** Baking soda + water or lemon juice

- **TOMATO (SAUCE, KETCHUP):** Vinegar + dish soap + cool water

A FEW GENERAL *tips*

Before treating your stain, always start by rinsing it out with lukewarm water from the reverse side of the fabric. This will help to push your stain right back out the way it came, rather than inviting it to get cozy deeper in the fibers of your fabric.

TIME IS OF THE ESSENCE!

When you see a stain, treat a stain. Or rather, treat it as soon as it's socially acceptable to do so. The less time the stain has to set up in your fabric, the easier it will be to get out.

TIME IS YOUR FRIEND!

If you've got a really tough stain on your hands (or your favorite shirt, rather) keep trying. If a little bit of soaking and treating doesn't work, just soak it for longer!

A lot of stains can be removed easily by using the super stain flush-out method. Place the stained area of your fabric over a big bowl with the reverse side up, or more importantly, with the side that was directly stained facing down. (So if you were wearing your clothes inside out that day for whatever strange reason, change these instructions up accordingly.) Take about 4 cups (950 ml) of warm water and pour it directly through the stain into the bowl. This is a new way of thinking about stain removal for a lot of people as you're physically pushing the stain out rather than removing it chemically or by rubbing it, but it really works well a lot of the time!

TEN THINGS YOUR MOM SHOULD HAVE TOLD YOU *about Housekeeping*

There are some housekeeping truths that have been passed down through the generations and still hold true today, and others maybe not so much. (Using the toilet plunger for cleaning socks? *Really?*) Trust the wisdom of your ancestors with the tips and tricks on this list, at least. Sometimes Mom really does know best!

TRUTH ONE

CLEANING IS AN EVERYDAY THING, NOT A ONCE-A-WEEK THING

At some point along the way, we all just seem to have stopped thinking about house cleaning as a daily thing, and we started trying to cram it all into one tiny little Saturday morning. Advancements in technology have definitely made certain tasks easier and quicker, but there's still a lot of peace of mind to be gained from keeping up with things daily and not letting the mess become overwhelming and disastrous before we take the time to deal with it.

TRUTH TWO

INVEST MORE IN YOUR CLEANING TOOLS THAN YOUR CLEANING PRODUCTS

A good-quality broom, mop, feather duster and vacuum cleaner can last you years or even a lifetime if you take care of them and will make your life so much easier. We seem to love the idea of a cheap quick-fix that a bottle of miracle cleaner promises us from its spot on the grocery store shelves, but as soon as you get some good-quality cleaning tools in your hands, you'll know that they're the real difference makers.

TRUTH THREE

YOU CAN PRETTY MUCH CLEAN EVERYTHING WITH VINEGAR

Not all store-bought cleaners are overrated, but 99 percent of them are. If you only have room to store one single cleaning product in your home, make it plain white vinegar. It really is good for almost anything.

TRUTH FOUR

CLEAN AS YOU GO

An ounce of prevention is worth a pound of cure! Always leave a room tidy when you're done with it and your home will always be tidy. It's as simple as that! Keeping a room clean and maintaining tidiness really takes only a tiny fraction of the overall time that it takes you to fix a giant disaster.

TRUTH FIVE

HOMEKEEPING IS AN ART

Homekeeping is important work and it deeply affects everyone in your home on many different levels. It is an art, but it's also a science and even a business. Past generations understood the importance of being a home manager and gave their housework the respect, time and care it needed. *And* they were admired for a job well done, as they should have been. Give your home and your work around the house the respect that it deserves and it will repay you endlessly every day.

TRUTH SIX

ESTABLISH ROUTINES THAT WORK FOR YOU AND THAT YOU ENJOY

Having routines for all your basic day-to-day housekeeping tasks allows you to put your housework into automatic mode. It's important that you set up your own routines that really work for *you* specifically rather than following someone else's daily routines. Once you get your routines in place, all the little necessities will start to feel like they just happen all on their own without you really ever having to think or worry about them. Let's be real: your brainpower has much better things to be used on than figuring out just when you're going to be able to unload the dishwasher.

TRUTH SEVEN

BREAK BIG JOBS DOWN INTO LITTLE BITE-SIZE PIECES

It's OK to get overwhelmed by big jobs or even jobs that just *seem* big because you just really don't want to do them. We all do! Break these jobs down into teeny-tiny, bite-size tasks until they no longer seem intimidating, then go about getting the tasks done one step at a time. As a bonus, breaking a job down makes it easy to delegate parts of it if you happen to have any helpers around that day!

TRUTH EIGHT

TAKE CARE OF YOURSELF FIRST

Don't let your cleaning and homemaking make you feel like you're being kept from something important that needs to be done. It's important to take care of yourself first, so that you're fully present and ready to give it your all without being distracted. Make sure you're fed, rested, hydrated and dressed comfortably so you can move through your day with confidence, no matter what the day brings. You'll do a better, faster job of everything overall and you'll feel more positive toward getting things done in your home in the long run.

TRUTH NINE

WORK SMARTER, NOT HARDER

You've heard this saying before, and it's still the best way to get things done today. Put some consideration into how you go about doing each task on your to-do list—like by reading this book!—and you'll find things will start to go much better for you much more quickly than just trying to work harder doing things the same old way.

TRUTH TEN

YOU'LL GET BETTER

You absolutely won't learn to be the world's best cleaner and homemaker overnight, no matter how much you want it. The good news is, though, that you will continue to get better and better at it, little by little, as long as you keep giving your homekeeping practices a bit of your focus, interest and time. There will always be new challenges, but these challenges will always bring new skills and wisdom to your homekeeping bag of tricks. If you're clever enough to pick up this book and try to expand your skill-set a little bit, then you're clever enough to be an amazing housekeeper before you know it!

BLINDINGLY CLEAN
Bathrooms

A bathroom that shines is like the jewel in the crown that is your home.

—Me, being terrible at poetry

OK, so maybe trying to get poetic about cleaning the bathroom isn't really the best idea. Actually, it's completely unnecessary. A shiny, clean bathroom speaks for itself and is such a point of satisfaction and delight for any proud homekeeper. Keep reading to find out my tips for becoming that proud homekeeper:

- First of all, always dust your bathroom before you start cleaning it with sprays and liquid cleaners. Bathrooms are dust magnets, and getting rid of most of the fuzz and dust first will make everything sparkle in half the time.

- Heating up your bathroom by about ten degrees before cleaning will double the effectiveness of your cleaners! Try running the shower for a few minutes before you start the cleaning and let the steam loosen the grime up for you a bit first.

- A tidy bathroom is so much easier and quicker to keep clean overall. Put everything away from counters and flat surfaces that you possibly can, except for the hand soap and any decorative items.

- Remove hard-water buildup from faucets and surrounding areas by soaking them in vinegar for an hour or so and then wiping clean. If your only affected area is right where the water comes out of the faucet, try filling a plastic bag with vinegar and then attaching it with a rubber band so that the problem area is submerged. If your hard-water deposits are everywhere, just soak a few rags in vinegar and let them sit right on top of the hard-water stains. Hard-water buildup will get worse and harder to remove with age, so try to keep up with this little shine-renewing routine fairly regularly.

- If you wish that you could use your bathroom mirror right after a shower, but find that it's always fogging up, try applying a layer of cheap shaving cream on mirrors and even glass shower doors after you've done your regular glass-cleaning routine. After applying, simply rub it off with a clean dry cloth until your mirror shines. Bam! No more foggy mirrors!

- Use canned air to blow dust and debris out of your bathroom fans quickly and easily.

- Use a glass water repellant meant for car windshields on your glass shower doors, and even on your bathroom mirrors, to prevent water spots from sticking and as another way to keep them from fogging up.

- Get rid of soap scum on glass shower doors or on shower walls by wiping them down with a damp, used dryer sheet. Instant de-scumming!

- Prevent rust stains in the shower by painting the bottoms of any metal containers with clear nail polish. The nail polish will protect the metal surface from coming into direct contact with water, so it will never rust in the first place.

- A paste of dishwashing liquid and baking soda will get even the scummiest tub sparkling clean. Scrub the tub down with a cloth dipped in the paste and then rinse!

- Unclog tub drains naturally by pouring ½ cup (103 g) of baking soda down your drain, followed by ½ cup (120 ml) of vinegar, then plugging it immediately. Leave it to sit for ten minutes or so then follow up by running the hot water. Do this regularly to prevent clogs as well.

- An old, clean mascara wand is the perfect size for cleaning hair and fur out of drains (and the wand grips particles securely). It's also a lot less horrifying than trying to reach in there with your fingers!

- If the idea of never having to scrub your shower sounds pretty great to you, try keeping a spare dish brush in the shower and giving the walls and tub a good swish while you're in there to keep any soap scum from having the chance to build up. You can use the kind with the reservoir for soap or just a plain brush—either will do the trick! Bonus points if you dry the shower stall with your towel once you're done drying off yourself!

- When it's time to wash your shower curtain liner, toss an old towel in the washing machine and the dryer along with it to help remove the soap scum more effectively.

- Keep the air moving to avoid too much dampness and the mold that can result. Open a window if you can, or at least keep the door to the bathroom open as well as the shower curtain after each shower if you have trouble with mold. Close the shower curtain once the interior of the shower is dry to let it air out as well.

- Pour a big bucket of water down your toilet before cleaning it. This will engage the flush mechanism and will drain your toilet bowl, but it won't refill until you flush the lever. Your cleaner will be able to work better because it will have more direct contact with a larger area of your toilet bowl.

- Clean stubborn toilet stains from hard water by using a pumice stone. It won't scratch the toilet but will remove the stains in a matter of seconds.

- Remove the toilet seat from the toilet and clean under it at least once every few months to really help keep the room smelling fresh. When you see how much stuff can collect under there, you'll be amazed . . . and probably a little grossed out, too.

- Rubbing alcohol is a great finishing touch to your bathroom cleaning routine. Wiping everything down with a cloth dampened with a little bit of rubbing alcohol will remove any residual oily films, make everything extra shiny and it has sanitizing properties as well!

- The bathroom is one of the areas of your home that really can benefit from a daily cleaning. Just a little each day goes a long way. A few wipes with a rag here, a little decluttering there and big bathroom deep-cleaning days will soon be a thing of the past.

HOW TO MAKE YOUR HOUSE LOOK LIKE YOU HAVE RIDICULOUSLY METICULOUS *Cleaning Standards*

You might not actually have time to clean every inch of your house with an old toothbrush and white gloves, but you can still make it look and feel like you do! In this chapter, I'll share some of the best tricks to get that "I spend every waking minute cleaning" look to your house.

Whether you want to impress your friends or just make it really abundantly clear to your husband/wife/kids/dog that you did in fact spend your whole day off at home cleaning and providing an amazingly welcoming home environment for them (and they should be grateful, dang it), there are always times where we really want people to *notice* all the hard work we've been putting in. Or all the hard work they *think* we've been putting in. Your choice. Of course, most of us tidy up and keep things bumping along pretty nicely in the everyday cleaning department (well, at least mostly), but we all know that a lot of those everyday things can go unnoticed. You know what I'm talking about. That dreaded "I swear I've been working all day, so why do I have nothing to show for it?" feeling. These tricks will give you a built-in "I was born to clean" appearance, whether everything really is spic-and-span, or whether you've been taking a day or three off from your regular cleaning routine.

LABEL EVERYTHING

There's something about seeing labels all around your house that just makes people think you're really on top of things house-wise (and life-wise, too). For some reason, we naturally think that an organized person is also a clean person. Therefore, a *really* organized person is also a *really* clean person. And a *really, really* in-your-face organized person is also a really, really . . . OK. I'll stop there. You get the picture. There really isn't a much better way to say, "Hey! Look at me! I'm super organized!" than tidy little labels, preferably printed out from a label maker or from the computer for that nice finishing touch. Of course, you'll get extra bonus points if you have your cleaning-supply storage area labeled, too! I love this tip because it's almost permanent. Once you label everything, you pretty much give off the impression of being totally on top of stuff to everyone who enters your home for the rest of eternity. As an added benefit, you'll probably start to *actually* be a little more organized, too—but for real.

TAKE IT EASY ON THE DEEP-CLEANING TASKS

Now, I definitely don't mean don't do them at all. In fact, after you read the following suggestions, you'll probably end up actually doing a lot *more* of those serious deep-cleaning tasks. You know, like when you take down every single curtain in the house, wash them all, iron them and hang them back up. And then no one notices, ever. Because unless you have gobs of dust from thirty-five years of total neglect, clean curtains don't really look much better than the ones that you just touch up with a vacuum every once in a while. But they *are* better for allergies if they're clean, and they definitely make you feel pretty impressed with yourself when you clean them. If you start and finish this task all in one go, though, you really run the risk of coming down with a case of working-all-day-with-nothing-to-show-for-it-itis yet again. So take it easy. Relax. Take your time.

This is where the cleverness comes in. Start the task, and then leave it out for the next day. It's a little bit life changing, actually, because it's pretty quick and easy to do a job like this only halfway and then walk away from it. *And* it lets you show off a little bit about what a fantastically detail-oriented housekeeper you are. So leave the clean curtains on the ironing board and don't hang them back up. Or leave them to soak in the washing machine overnight. Don't wait for the fact that you cleaned the curtains today to come up in casual conversation, because really, who talks about that over dinner? Just let it be seen that it was done and is, in fact, in the process of happening. You don't even have to mention it. You'll know that they know. Oh, yes, they'll know. And that just might be all the motivation you need to wash your curtains regularly from now on. Or to clean all your glass light fixtures. Or vacuum all the window screens. If you've been known to avoid these bigger jobs because no one really notices, then chances are that anyone else that comes into your home does that very same thing. And they'll be pretty impressed at what a neat freak you must be. And you can either tell them your little "take it easy" secret or you can just let them go on admiring you in all your neat-freaked glory. I'll leave that one up to you.

DECORATE USING CLEAN COLORS

The moment I started giving the trim in my main rooms a nice fresh coat of white semigloss and started using my favorite warm gray on my walls, my house suddenly became sixty-seven times cleaner in people's eyes. Believe me, our house is *lived in* and we have all the spills, smears and "oopsies" that every house with kids and other humans has. So why would anyone in their right mind be afraid to even accept a cup of coffee in my living room for fear of messing it up?

The first time I had my neighbor and her baby girl over to my house, I assumed that she just didn't drink coffee or eat banana bread and that I'd been a little rude in planning to offer only those things to them for our morning playdate. I found out weeks later that she'd been too afraid to spill anything in my "beautifully clean" living room, so she just didn't have any. I've since learned that this girl loves her coffee and her food, so this is really saying something. I couldn't figure out why in the world she would think that my thoroughly toddlerfied living room would ever be somewhere that a spill would be a big deal. I realized that it was all in the colors! I knew that as soon as I painted the room, I definitely *felt* like it was cleaner in there, so I kept adding in more of the fresh grays and shiny whites that just made me feel happy over and over again. Obviously, it wasn't just my own impression and that color scheme really does provide a "built-in cleanliness" to the room as similar things have happened in my other clean-colored rooms since then. I'll tell you all about them the next time you're over for coffee, but for now here are some clean-looking colors to add into your decor scheme:

- Soft grays

- Crisp, glossy whites

- Light blue-grays

- Navy blues

- Aqua blues

- Fresh greens with a bit of yellow to them

- Very soft yellows (these can also give off a clean vibe, but they can be a little trickier to get right)

USE SYMMETRY

Something about having objects placed symmetrically really attracts the eye and allows it to rest there, just for a moment. This can work to your benefit for a couple of reasons. To an extent, you're controlling where the eyeballs in your room are looking, so they're noticing your pretty vases on the mantel or those two matching chairs on either side of the coffee table and not necessarily the corners that haven't been vacuumed quite as often lately or that book shelf that's getting a little too full to dust properly. Symmetry in a room is also just one of those little tricks that gives off the impression that you're really in control of everything in your home and that you must be extra meticulous about it since you obviously like to have everything *just so*.

OWN A FEATHER DUSTER

Nothing says "I'm going to clean it like I mean it" in a really serious, old-school kind of way like a traditional feather duster. Feather dusters seem to have gotten a reputation as kind of finicky little things that are only for people with a lot of time on their hands for cleaning and pretending that they're super fancy. The truth is, though, that good-quality feather dusters do an incredibly effective job of picking up dust in even the hardest-to-reach places with almost zero effort on your part. It's so easy to walk around your house, making everything sparkle and shine in just a few minutes. I've always thought feather dusters were sort of like the original cleaning "hack." They make a really tedious job easy—and actually kinda fun! And yes, you do in fact look pretty fancy with one in your hand.

ALWAYS MAKE YOUR BED

You've probably heard this one before. In fact, if you've already read "The Single Most Important Habit that You Need to Start Doing Right Away" (page 30), then I know you have! Nothing makes a bedroom look tidy and taken care of more quickly than just making your bed. If you're worried about someone walking down the hallway on their way to the bathroom and seeing just how messy your life really is, making your bed will completely change their perspective. Conversely, *not* making your bed will absolutely give people the impression that you're a little sloppy when it comes to housekeeping, no matter how spotless the rest of your house is. It's so easy and the payoff is huge! Just do it.

GET CAUGHT IN THE ACT

If you really want to give off the "master housekeeper" vibe, then letting people actually see you in the act of cleaning can really make them associate you with the idea of cleaning. I'm not talking about getting on your hands and knees and scrubbing the grout with a toothbrush, because let's face it, that would just be awkward. But don't hesitate to grab a cloth and wipe down a few surfaces here and there like you normally would or to tidy up a room for a few seconds as you enter into it. This might seem a little too calculated, but for those times when you really want to send the message that "Hey, I've got this housekeeping thing down," getting caught in the act of cleaning can really put an exclamation mark on all your other efforts.

SHINE ON

A little bit of sparkle goes a long way
to making your home look its most polished. Here are some tricks for getting all
your glass, mirrors and lustrous things of luminosity their shiniest in a flash!

MIRRORS

We all seem to be looking for that one perfect tool or cleaning product that will
make our mirrors streak-free and brilliant 100 percent of the time, but the truth
is that it just doesn't exist. I've found that the best way to really clean mirrors is
more of a one-two punch. First, use your cleaner on the mirrors. I love to use a
little dab of rubbing alcohol on a stack of a few coffee filters. The rubbing alcohol
really cleans and evaporates perfectly and the coffee filters grab all the debris
and fogginess and don't leave any lint behind. After that, I like to take a dry
microfiber cloth to give everything a nice final polish. Does the trick every time!

INTERIOR WINDOWS

If mirrors need the one-two punch approach, then window cleaning is more like a punch-punch-jab-kick type of method. First, dust off the windowsills and trim and vacuum out the tracks. Next, take a rag with warm soapy water and wash the entire window area, including any vinyl or wood parts of the window frame and the glass itself. Finish up by polishing everything just like a mirror with the rubbing alcohol, coffee filters and microfiber cloth.

SILVER

Keep your silver looking its best by polishing it every few months to keep a heavy layer of tarnish from building up. The easiest method is to do a big batch of silver polishing all at once. Line a sink or a big bowl with aluminum foil with the shiny side up, add all your silver pieces then sprinkle everything with about a cup (206 g) of baking soda. Fill the sink or bowl up with really hot water and leave it to sit until the water cools down. Take everything out and wipe away any leftover tarnish with a soft, dry cloth.

BRASS

For heavily tarnished brass, make a paste of lemon juice and baking soda and use it to clean the brass with a soft cloth. For everyday touch-ups, a little wax-based furniture polish on a soft cloth does the trick!

ELECTRONICS

We tend to forget about our electronics when we're focused on cleaning our decorative items and they can become caked in dust and fingerprints pretty quickly, making our homes feel dirty without us even noticing! Keep your electronics looking shiny and new by dusting them on all sides regularly with a good feather duster and touching up where it's needed on screens and solid plastic pieces with a basic glass cleaner. For areas with buttons and hard-to-reach places, a cotton swab dipped in rubbing alcohol works amazingly well.

DECORATIVE GLASS AND CERAMICS

A lot of glass and ceramic objects actually look better the less you handle them because there is less build up of streaks and fingerprints, so a good swipe with your feather duster on a regular basis is usually all they need. When it's time to give them a good cleaning every once in a while, it helps to wear cheap, thin winter gloves while you're giving them a wipe-down with a damp cloth or some glass cleaner. The gloves keep you from leaving fingerprints and actually give whatever you're handling a nice little extra polish!

WOOD FURNITURE

Wood furniture should be polished on a regular basis to keep it healthy and happy and to make sure it enjoys a long and beautiful life. Whether you use a store-bought polish or one you make yourself, just remember that a little goes a long way and to always use a very soft cloth to avoid scratching. You can make your own furniture polish by combining ½ cup (120 ml) of olive oil with ¼ cup (60 ml) of lemon juice. Store it in the fridge between uses.

GRANITE

For regular daily maintenance of your granite counters (or other granite finery), wipe them down with warm soapy water and follow up with rubbing alcohol to disinfect and really make them shine. Never use lemon juice or vinegar to clean granite, since the acidity in these products can eat away at that beautiful, shiny stone!

MARBLE

Marble is pretty similar to granite only it's much softer and much more susceptible to staining. Just like with granite, never use any acidic cleaners because they will cause etching marks immediately (as will any acidic foods that drop on the surface). So, just some nice soap and water will do the trick. For any stains that seep their way into the surface of your marble, you can remove them using a paste of baking soda, dish soap and a little water. Apply the paste directly to the stain, cover it in plastic wrap to keep it moist and leave it to sit for a day or so to draw the stain out.

CERAMIC TILE

If your tiles are looking a little hazy, clean them with a mild acid, like lemon juice mixed with water, to bring them back to their former shiny glory. Clean grout is also key to making your overall tile experience its very best. Clean any stained grout with a paste of baking soda and water. Leave the paste to sit overnight for stubborn stains.

CHROME

It's pretty easy to make chrome look spectacularly shiny using a basic microfiber cloth and a little bit of water, but if your chrome has a bit of rust buildup on it, grab a can of cola as your cleaner of choice. Apply the cola to a soft cloth and then slop it onto the rust liberally. Next, grab a ball of aluminum foil and use that to scrub the rust away. The aluminum foil will scour the rust off easily, but won't scratch the chrome one bit!

BRUSHED METALS

Brushed metals do well with a vinegar-and-water solution for a cleaner. Follow up with a wax-based furniture polish to protect them and make them easier to clean on a daily basis.

OIL-RUBBED BRONZE AND OTHER DARK METALS

Dark metals can be a really stunning accent in any room, but they're also notorious for showing dust and fingerprints. I really love to give my dark metals a nice deep color by using furniture polish on them when I can, but if the metal is an accent to a glass light fixture or something similar, then it's a bad idea to use oil or wax-based cleaners. In that case, good old glass cleaner will usually do the trick. Although I love to use rubbing alcohol on glass, I avoid using it directly on the dark metal parts because they're sometimes actually painted and the rubbing alcohol can take the paint right off.

STAINLESS STEEL

Stainless steel is a very popular metal and something a lot of people have in their homes these days. There are a lot of great cleaning solutions that you can use on surfaces made out of stainless steel, so find which one works best for you. Generally, anything you would use to make something shine will work on most stainless steels, but you'll need to experiment as there are many different shine-levels and grains to different stainless steel products. Some great ones to try include regular glass cleaner, furniture polish, water with a microfiber cloth and baby oil.

PLASTICS, ACRYLICS AND RESINS

Plastics are cheap, easy to care for and often look as nice in a home as their heavier, more expensive counterparts. For the most part, care for these items the same way as you would glass or ceramic—just make sure you take extra care not to scratch them, as they can lose their shine and their appeal pretty easily.

THE SECRET CLEANING ROBOTS THAT YOU ALREADY
Have in Your Home

It's true! Your own little miracle cleaning machines have been right there under your nose the whole time! No, you probably weren't visited in the night by aliens who dropped off the Clean-O-Matic 7000 from the future, but you *do* have some pretty powerful hands-free cleaning devices right there, just waiting for you to use them, in the form of your handy-dandy dishwasher and laundry machines. Here are a few clever ways to use them that you probably haven't thought of before.

CLEVER CLEANING WITH THE DISHWASHER

Your dishwasher can do so much more to help you out besides just washing your dishes! Check out the following list of a few ideas for what you can clean in your dishwasher to get you started. I bet you can come up with even more dishwashable items in your home, though, if you have a look around!

ITEMS THAT CAN BE CLEANED IN YOUR DISHWASHER

- Vacuum attachments

- Doorknobs

- Outlet covers

- Window screens

- Vent grates

- Small trash cans

- Refrigerator bins and trays

- Glass parts from light fixtures

- Plastic combs and hairbrushes

- Soap trays, toothbrush holders and other bathroom accessories

- Plastic toys

- Cleaning tools and brushes

- Toothbrushes

- Hair clips

- Baseball hats

- Sink stoppers

- Basic tools

- Gardening tools

- Fake plants and flowers

- Desk accessories

- Storage containers and organizers

- Drawer knobs and cabinet door pulls

A FEW *guidelines* TO REMEMBER

If you've never washed an item from the list in the dishwasher before, use your lowest temperature setting and place it on the top rack the first time you try it—if it can fit on the top rack.

Don't wash these items along with your regular load of dishes for the most part. Use your common sense!

Use your load of clever goods as an excuse to do your regular dishwasher cleaning cycle as outlined in "The Cleanest Kitchen on the Block" (page 38). Just run the cleaning cycle right after you're done washing all the unusual things. That way, you've got a fresh, clean dishwasher for your next load of dishes and a dishwasher that continues to run smoothly for a long time to come, no matter what you put in it!

Place smaller items in the utensil rack or place them in a mesh bag on the top rack.

Some items might do better to be cleaned with just 1 cup (240 ml) of vinegar placed on the top rack of the dishwasher rather than with standard dishwashing detergent.

CLEVER CLEANING USING YOUR LAUNDRY MACHINES

Your washing machine and dryer can be some pretty intense cleaning environments, but sometimes that's just exactly what you need. Next, you'll find a list of some things that you can clean better and more easily by just plunking them in your washing machine!

ITEMS THAT CAN BE CLEANED IN YOUR LAUNDRY MACHINES

- Stuffed animals

- Pillows

- Couch cushion covers

- Shoes and slippers

- LEGOs (in a mesh bag)

- Rugs

- Curtains

- Backpacks and lunch bags

- High-chair and car-seat covers

- Shower curtains (even the plastic ones)

- Car mats

- Yoga mats

- Chair cushions

- Bath toys

SOME *guidelines* TO REMEMBER

Because the washing machine shakes and churns your stuff around, consider it to be one step up in cleaning intensity compared to your dishwasher.

Use the cold water setting the first time you wash something unusual in your washing machine if your common sense tells you to. Cold water equals a gentler washing experience and less risk of damage.

You can keep items like shoes from clunking around too much by first placing them in an old pillowcase and then tying it loosely to keep it closed.

Use caution when mixing loads of unusual items with regular laundry. Check for hooks, zippers and other things on your "clever laundry items" that may become stuck on delicate fabrics from your everyday clothing wash load.

THE GREAT
(OR SOMETIMES
NOT-SO-GREAT)
Outdoors

Our outdoor spaces don't always measure up to the inside area of our homes when it comes to cleanliness and tidiness. You're dealing with a whole slew of different challenges out there along with all the regular dirt and dust that you get inside, so to truly make your outdoor area just as comfortable and livable as indoors, you might need to have a few extra-strength tricks up your sleeve. Here are some of the best that will help you make quick work of all your outdoor jobs!

CLEANING OUTDOOR WINDOWS

Keeping the outdoor side of windows clean and sparkly can be such a challenge, especially if your house is out in the dusty, buggy country like ours is. If your windows have a lot of dirt and cobweb buildup, start by removing most of it with an old broom. Next, you'll want to follow up with a good, strong spray from your garden hose or pressure washer. Make a cleaning solution of about 1 gallon (3.6 L) of water, 1 tablespoon (15 ml) of dishwashing liquid and 1 tablespoon (15 ml) of dishwasher rinse aid and apply it to your window using a soft long-handled brush. Rinse the cleaner off immediately with a spray from the hose, then use a squeegee to pull all the extra water off of your window, wiping the squeegee with a cloth after each swipe. If you find that you have a buildup of white water spots on your windows from past cleaning attempts with hard water, you can clean them away pretty easily with a mixture of half vinegar and half water before you start with your regular window cleaning routine as I described above. Going forward, your game plan will be all about preventing as much window unpleasantness as possible. I like to use a spider spray around my windows and doors about once a month during the summer to discourage them from building their webs right on top of my windows, and that goes a long way toward keeping my view clear. Some people also swear by using an automotive-glass water repellant on their house windows to help the rain water just sheet off cleanly.

CLEANING VINYL SIDING

Exterior vinyl siding is incredibly resilient when it comes to dealing with the elements, and it really does give your home a crisp, clean look year after year, asking for very little in return. Its one downfall, however, is that it can become covered in moss and mold pretty easily in areas that don't get much sunlight. Of course, since the rest of your house looks so fresh and clean, these areas stand out all that much more. If this scenario sounds familiar to you, I'd strongly recommend investing in a good pressure washer with a nice long cord. Actually, even a smaller economical pressure washer will really help you significantly and will allow you to clean your house without having to use any strong chemical cleaners. Get your pressure washer set up, find the attachment that gives you the strongest spray and get to spraying! Be sure to keep a long-handled scrub brush nearby for any really difficult spots. The key to getting this job done efficiently lies not so much in the "how" but more so in the "how often." If you can spend a few hours on the dirtiest parts of your siding once each spring and again each fall, then icky green siding will be something that you never have to worry about again.

DECK AND PATIO MAINTENANCE

Whether your deck is a brand-new dream entertaining space or it's older and more basic, a little bit of love and maintenance will go a long way toward how it looks and how much you enjoy using it. Wooden decks (as well as concrete, brick and stone patios) all need to be kept clean and protected from the elements as much as possible. Pressure wash your deck or patio as often as you would wash your siding and use a sealant made for your particular type of decking material once every one to two years. Avoid harsh chemical deck cleaners as most of them are pretty much just a bottle of bleach and totally unnecessary. If you need a little more power to get your deck sparkly clean, just use some warm water, a little bit of dish soap and a stiff, long-handled scrub brush and you'll be good to go!

WASHING OUTDOOR FURNITURE

Buildup from dust, grime and pollution can start to eat away at the finish of your outdoor furniture pretty quickly. When you add in the exposure to the sun, wind and constantly changing temperatures, it's actually pretty impressive that our outdoor furniture ever lasts more than one season! If you've ever left your patio furniture outside for an entire year and then compared it to how it looked when you first bought it, then you know that things can start to go downhill pretty fast. But the good news is that a little bit of upkeep will keep things looking up! Outdoor furniture should have a gentle spray-down and a thorough wiping with a soft cloth at least once a week during the warmer months and should stay stored indoors during the cold months if you live somewhere with harsh winters. Inspect the finish on your furniture at least once per season and repaint, restain or reseal as necessary. Even metal furniture will be really happy to have a protective topcoat every once in a while to prevent rusting. Fabric umbrellas, pillows and seat cushions need to be brought indoors when you're not using them—even if they're made of outdoor fabric—or they'll fade quickly. These things can take up a lot of space, so it's a good idea to set aside a dedicated storage area for your outdoor fabric things before the season begins, or you'll probably fail miserably at being disciplined when it comes to bringing them indoors. If you can spend just a few minutes caring for your outdoor furniture every week, though, it will last you through many a cocktails-on-the-patio season and will really help you make the most of your outdoor spaces.

WEEDS

Weeds are probably the biggest culprit when it comes to making our outdoor spaces look untidy and unloved, especially during the warmer months. Prevention is absolutely the key to winning this battle (especially if you happen to be someone who doesn't have sixteen free hours each day for pulling weeds). Make sure that all garden areas where you have open soil exposed to the air are covered in a thick layer of mulch and reapply it every few weeks to keep things looking fresh and to stifle any new weed growth. If this sounds like a bit of an expensive endeavor, check out your local recycling center. They may have mulch made from local tree clippings and yard waste available for free to local residents! That program is a complete lifesaver for me. Or a garden-saver, rather. Also check driveways and patios for cracks where weeds grow and fill all cracks with a driveway crack sealer, or polymeric sand, which creates kind of a "grout" between patio stones when it's exposed to water. Although there will still be a few weeds that will find places to grow in your lawn or in your garden, for the most part they won't make your home look completely neglected. If you can keep your hardscape areas weed-less, your gardens freshly mulched and your lawn freshly mowed, you're going to come off looking like a pretty handy-dandy gardener. For the few weeds that do pop-up in the wrong place here and there, a little bit of vinegar poured on the weed on a hot sunny day or even some table salt (only in areas where no other plants need to grow) will take care of the problem within a few hours. *And*, although weeds are generally thought to be pests, don't forget that some weeds are really just wildflowers in disguise and are actually quite beautiful, so as long as your outdoor spaces look tidy and well-loved, try to keep the weed-worrying to a minimum.

PESTS (LIKE, ACTUAL PESTS)

We all love that getting outside in our yards allows us to be a bit closer to nature and to experience a little wildlife, along with all the wonders of the bugs and the birds out there doing their thing. Even for the most adamant nature lover though, there's a line and sometimes that line gets crossed. Ants in your kids' sandbox? No thanks! Spider webs all over your favorite deck chair? Ick! If you can just let all these little critters know where they're welcome and where they're not before they even get there, your relationship with all the other life out in your yard can be much more harmonious, and you may even start to see them as welcome visitors here and there, rather than pests. Here are a few tips for discouraging common outdoor pests:

ANTS

Many strongly scented herbs and spices smell amazing to us but absolutely repulsive to ants. Try mixing cinnamon or cloves into your sandbox or even sprinkling it around flower gardens or walkways that you want them to steer clear of. Sage or bay leaves have also been known to work well for this purpose.

(continued)

SPIDERS

Depending on where you live and what kind of spiders live there with you, having too many spiders in the wrong places can be anywhere from mildly icky to downright dangerous! One easy thing you can do is to minimize the use of outdoor lights at night. The lights attract bugs that are food for the spiders, so if you have your porch light on, then your porch is exactly where the spiders will set up shop. You also want to make sure that you keep the spider-prone area fairly minimally decorated and furnished, with wide spaces between any flower pots and surrounding walls, as the little cracks and crevices created by lots of stuff are cozy little spider hiding spots. The most effective method is probably to get a good basic household indoor/outdoor spider spray. Spraying down an area once a month or so is usually enough to discourage most spiders from visiting that spot.

SLUGS

Slugs love a moist, cool climate, so chances are that if you have slug issues, you live somewhere that gets a lot of rain or you have a very shady yard. Simply keeping your garden area drier can really help. Space plants out in your garden to allow sunlight between your plants, water your plants in the morning so that your garden can dry out before nightfall, and try using underground irrigation hoses so you use less water overall and the water goes directly to the roots of your plants rather than creating a damp environment at the soil's surface. Some people also swear by creating a little ring of coffee grounds or coarse sand around the base of their plants to make it really uncomfortable for the slugs to crawl in that area.

MOSQUITOS

Just like slugs, mosquitos love damp, shady areas. They also reproduce in standing water and actually need very little of it to set up their tiny homes of terror. The old trick of making sure the water in your birdbath is fresh isn't going to cut it. If you have saucers under your potted plants, kids' toys or even a barbecue cover that collects water when it rains, those are all great breeding spots for mosquitos as well. It takes about eight days for mosquito eggs to hatch, so if you make sure to tip the standing water out of all of these areas at least once a week, you'll make a big difference right there. You can refill with fresh water again right afterwards if needed for your plants. Keeping your yard sunny and dry really helps overall and will even help decrease the number of mosquitos you see in the evening hours as the sun starts to go down.

RABBITS AND OTHER PLANT EATERS

Most of these sneaky—but cute, let's admit it—creatures are pretty timid and like to have somewhere nearby to hide just in case they think they might be spotted. Try not to have a lot of shrubbery or piles of stones or wood near your garden and you'll have won half the battle. Most garden nibblers prefer younger plant shoots when they're available, so if you really step up your efforts to keep them away early in the season, then you'll be in good shape once the plants mature and become a little tougher. For the most part, protecting your young springtime plants is the name of the game, so you may need to install temporary fencing or some garden fabric over the plants that seem to be getting eaten the most for a little while. Luckily, there are lots of different options coming out all the time as this is a pretty common problem. Look for pop-up plant tents, easy-to-use hoop systems to hold garden fabric or good ol' wire fencing to keep your gardens safe.

THE FINISHING TOUCHES

Just like when you're trying to make your indoor spaces seem fresh and inviting, the finishing touches can make such a big difference. Once you have the basics down of somewhere to sit and somewhere to put your drink, it can be hard to know what else to add that will be both practical for the outdoors and easy to keep clean and maintain throughout the outdoor season. Luckily, it doesn't take much other than a little knowledge and a little bit of experience to give your space an extra bit of polish. Fewer, larger planters will be much easier to care for than many small ones, and you'll get bonus points for polish if you can find two matching ones to place on either side of a door or walkway. Keep decorative outdoor accessories to a minimum, too, and use the same rule of fewer larger pieces rather than many smaller ones. Lots of small decorative accessories everywhere can actually make your patio space feel outdated and neglected pretty quickly—it can seem like you haven't taken the time to get rid of anything for years and have simply been adding new things on top of the old. Outdoor spaces feel the most comfortable when the focus is on plants and greenery, so add just a few pillows in outdoor fabric that you love for any seating areas and, of course, one or two items with a bit of shine, and you'll be amazed at how fresh and new your space feels, even if you only do minimal cleaning all season long.

HOW
TO BE
A Cleaning Ninja

OK, so I won't have you scaling twenty-foot (six-meter) walls or jumping over rivers in a single bound, but I will have you *feeling* like a bit of a ninja, at least when it comes to cleaning your home. If you can mix up your routine a little and play a few games while accomplishing your goals, you'll find that your energy and focus will be supercharged. You'll be amazed at just how many things you can check off your list in just a short amount of time, all while actually enjoying yourself. Here are some of my favorite little games and tactics that make me feel like I have superhuman speed and agility when I need it most around the house.

For when you keep seeing little jobs around the house that make you say, "I should really do that soon. Maybe a little later . . . "

THE "TEN TIMES TWO"

Grab a piece of paper and a pen (or open up the notepad on your phone), and take a little walk around your house. Take note of each little two-minute-ish job that catches your eye and write it down as its own bullet point on your list. These jobs will probably be things like putting stuff away, wiping things down or organizing small areas. You might be surprised to find that you'll need to get a bit creative near the end to find ten things to fill up your list. That means that not only do you get all the stuff that's bugging you done, you also get a few bonus things done, too. Look at you—you're on a roll! Once your list is filled in, set your timer on your phone or your oven for two minutes and complete the first task. It may take a few seconds more or a few seconds less, and that's OK. When the first little task is done, reset your timer and move on to the next one. You'll feel so speedy for getting so many things done in twenty-or-so minutes that you may even want to keep going!

For when you have a big holiday, event or project coming up that you're planning for and you need to somehow get all the stuff done for that but also keep up with your regular housework . . .

THE "WATCH ME PULL A NUMBER OUT OF MY HAT"

Make a list of five different jobs, including a few basic household tasks that you need to keep up with and get done that day (laundry or vacuuming the stairs for instance) and a few that help you get stuff done for your event (like wrapping gifts or filling birthday loot bags) and label them each with the numbers 1–5. Next, tear up five tiny pieces of paper, write *1, 2, 3, 4* or *5* on each and stick them in a bowl. You'll draw each number out of the bowl and complete each job, giving yourself ten minutes to complete it. If you're not done, well, at least you've made progress! You'll be surprised at all you can get done in ten minutes, though, when you're truly doing only one thing. The random unpredictability of choosing the numbers from the bowl keeps you from getting distracted by the next job and from getting overwhelmed by all that you need to do, because you just don't know what's coming up next! Completing tasks from more than one area of your to-do list keeps you from feeling like you spent too much time on birthday party planning and not enough time on the real, necessary everyday tasks that you need to get done to keep your head above water.

For when you're feeling pulled in multiple directions at the same time by competing priorities . . .

THE "LITTLE BIT OF THIS, LITTLE BIT OF THAT"

Sometimes you just feel like the most important thing that needs to get done right away is one thing and *also* another thing, too. Or maybe there are three things that you need to be working on, like, *right now*. The problem with making a single choice in that situation is that when we complete one big job from start to finish, we often feel like we've worked *really* hard at the end of it. And we feel like we deserve a break. Just like when you fold four loads of laundry all at once. It's not really a big deal, but it's still pretty tiring. The problem with taking a break at the end of completing your job is that you're only giving yourself more stress in the future. Pretty soon, you remember those other things that you really needed to get done two hours ago and now you're wondering what you're going to do. So when you start to notice that this is the direction your day or your evening is taking, then grab a timer, set it for five minutes and work on a little bit of your first competing priority job. When the five minutes are up, move on to the next chore. Then move on to the next one again if you have three of these types of tasks *or* just go back to the first one. This way, you're making steady progress on all of your tasks essentially at the same time. *And* the neat thing is that a lot of the time you'll get two or three tasks done in the amount of time that it would normally take you to complete just one! When you work in small five-minute bursts, you don't have time to get bored and distracted (and slow!) like you do when you work on something for an hour straight!

For those tedious jobs that you just. Can't. *Bring yourself to do today . . .*

THE "TWO-MINUTE SWITCH-OUT"

For when you really just feel like yelling, "But I don't waaanna!" try this instead. Maybe you can't stand the thought of working on that particular job for an hour, or half an hour, or however long you think it's going to take to get done, but you can do two minutes, right? You can do anything for two minutes. So set your timer for two minutes and then get to work. When the timer goes off, go do something else and then come back and do two minutes on the dreaded task again. You'll be motivated by being able to see results after only two teeny-weeny minutes (and you *will* see results, always), and you'll probably be surprised at how few two-minute sessions it will take to get the job done pretty much painlessly. Bonus: you'll get a whole bunch of other stuff done during your in-between session times, and you'll keep yourself moving rather than getting stuck in lazy procrastination-ville.

For when you're super-tired . . .

THE "EASY DOES IT"

So what about when *everything* seems like too much? When you know you need to get moving but you just want to go to bed? Or watch seventeen hours straight of TV? Well, this is the one time when I say *not* to make a list. Or, rather, don't make a list right away. You need to be extra nice to yourself sometimes, and this is one of those times, so you need to get up on your feet, start walking around your house and find one ridiculously easy thing to do. And do it. Something so easy that you think you could pretty much get it done while sleeping. And then do that again. You'll soon start to feel better and more energized, and you'll probably even be enjoying your relaxed cleaning a little bit. *Then* you can start to make your list and get working on it. When you feel like it. If not, keep going with the walking around and the easy stuff–doing. Whatever you do, just don't flop back down on the couch. Not only will you not regain your energy that way (even though I know you think you will!), but you'll also be forcing yourself to deal with your mounting guilt over not getting stuff done.

For when you have a whole day free to get stuff done but you can't seem to focus . . .

THE "INSTANT PAYOFF"

You have a whole day ahead of you and you have big plans! So why can't you get started? Sometimes it can be hard to know where to start in a day when you have so much going on and so much potentially awesome productivity on the radar. You need to get yourself motivated and you need to get yourself excited about all the possibility that opens up when you just. Get. Stuff. Done. So sit down with a cup of tea and replan that day, starting with the task with the highest payoff first. The one that will make you say, "Yes! I'm so glad I got that done!" or, "Look how amazing this room looks now! I'm *so* glad I tackled this!" That feeling of accomplishment becomes just a tiny bit addictive, and soon you can't stop yourself from checking off all kinds of jobs from your list. Our natural inclination can be to save the big payoff for the end of the day and to get the tedious stuff out of the way first, but what you need is momentum. Get those jobs that make you feel like a superstar done first and you'll just breeze through the tedious stuff later on in the day!

For those big jobs you keep putting off . . .

THE "ELEPHANT EATER"

How do you eat an elephant?

One bite at a time!

We've all heard this saying before, but somehow we keep forgetting it. If you have something big that you'd like to accomplish, like a file cabinet with twenty-five years' worth of papers to clean out or a guest room that has become the dumping ground for all of your homeless items, it's pretty easy to put off tackling that job "until you have the time." Which is never. Who has a whole week to dedicate to something like that all at once? The rest of your world would be a disaster after that and that's not helping anyone! So you do the responsible thing: you just ignore it and carry on with your life. Keeping everything else afloat. If this sounds like you (and it probably does because we all have an area like this in our home somewhere), I've got the magic ticket to freedom from these nagging jobs hanging over your head! You're going to do one "bite" at a time! You need to decide what one bite is for you because you're the one who has been putting this off for so long and you're the only one who knows why exactly you dread this job so much. Your "bite" could be a measurement of time that feels comfortable to you and like something that you can easily fit into your day—say, five minutes. Or one shelf. Or putting away one item. Whatever feels reasonable to you. The thing is, it doesn't matter what your bite is, as long as you take it! Before long, that elephant of yours is going to start to taste downright delicious!

Are you ready to take on the world—or at least your messy house—with mind-boggling speed and agility? I can answer that for you. Yes! Yes, you are!

When you think of ninjas, you think of small stealthy moves that are so tiny they're almost undetectable, yet they make a huge impact. That's exactly the way you'll be going about your housework if you give these little challenges a try. You'll be achieving so much in such a small amount of time each day—and you'll be makin' it look easy, too!

HOME
SCENTS
That Make Sense

Fact: a home that smells fresh, clean and inviting *feels* 93.7 percent more fresh, clean and inviting. But with so many options available for creating a great-smelling home, it can be overwhelming and hard to know which is the best one to choose. As with most things, the simplest options are usually the best ones. Here are a few ideas and pointers for making sure that your home always smells its best.

GET RID OF THOSE BAD ODORS

Whether your home stench is coming from cooking smells, pets or just general staleness, there are some easy things that you can do to eliminate those pesky odors without cleaning your house from top to bottom. It's better to get rid of odors first before you add other pleasant aromas than to try to just skip forward to the good smells and mask your stinkiness.

KEEP THINGS CLEAN

Now, I know I just finished saying that you don't need to always clean your house top to bottom to get rid of your unpleasant smells. But let's be real—keeping things decently clean on a regular basis will definitely help keep things smelling a little fresher. Pay attention to your carpets, draperies and upholstery, which can hold odors in them without you really realizing it.

KEEP THINGS MOVING

Drains and appliances, like washing machines, dishwashers and even ovens and microwaves that go a long time between uses can start to get a really weird smell to them. Try to use most of these things in your home on most days or give them a good wipeout if you know they won't be in use for a while.

OPEN A WINDOW

Maybe it seems a little *too* obvious, but this quick-fix is also often forgotten. Give your whole house that "fresh laundry off the line" treatment and let the fresh air wash over everything. That fresh-laundry scent that we love so much is really just an absence of scent and our noses are so used to being filled with all kinds of odors and smells that we find the lack of scent in fresh laundry to be such incredible aromatherapy, or no-romatherapy, treatment!

NEVER UNDERESTIMATE THE POWER OF BAKING SODA

You overlook good ol' baking soda because it's old-fashioned, basic and lacks that fancy packaging that comes with all of your other modern-day cleaning products. But when it comes to odor eliminators, it's just the best, hands down. Buy it by the cartload and use it pretty much everywhere.

ADD SOME AMBIANCE WITH A GREAT SCENT

Once you've neutralized any unpleasant odors lurking around your home, try adding in a bit of a fresh scent with one of these methods listed below. Home scents add great ambiance to your space and also boost your mood, enhance your energy levels and somehow make your whole home seem cleaner and fresher!

SCENTED CANDLES

To me, there's nothing like a good scented candle to transform how my home feels almost instantly. Even if I've just finished a mini cleaning spree and everything is spic and span, the feeling of freshness is still always enhanced by a nice light fragrance from a candle. It's like the finishing touch on all my hard work. Or, I light a candle *before* starting in on a cleaning job to give me a sense of progress on the level of freshness in my home right away. It's best to go with higher-quality candles over cheap ones because the scents will be stronger and much more enjoyable. Cheaper candles are also typically made with cheaper ingredients that you really don't want to be breathing in on a regular basis.

ROOM SPRAYS

Room sprays are great when you need a little scent boost around your home in a flash (or in the bathroom, where a lot of people use them). I almost always run around and spray the main rooms of our home whenever I know someone will be coming over, not because my house is really stinky but because I just like to be sure that it's at its absolute freshest before I invite people in. You never really know for sure if there's a lingering smell that you've gotten used to because you've been in your house all day without stepping outside for some fresh air. I like to use the specialty highly concentrated room sprays that you can often get from companies who focus on fragrance rather than the cheaper grocery-store types, because you usually only need a tiny amount of spray to get a pleasant fragrance. There's no need to stand in the middle of the room spinning and spraying for minutes on end, like you've seen them do in the commercials.

STOVE TOP

Scenting your home by simmering a pot of water on your stovetop is one of the most economical and natural ways that you can do it. It can be as simple as tossing in a few herbs and spices. Or you can even chop up fresh herbs and fruits, freeze them in little ready-to-go packs and use them whenever the mood strikes. You can also use up citrus peels or even evergreen branches from your yard, but whatever you do, make sure that your pot is attended at all times and you don't allow it to boil down to nothing or you could have a fire on your hands—or at least a very unpleasant smoky smell. Here are some classic stovetop scent combinations to try if this sounds right up your alley:

- Orange peels and whole or ground cloves

- Cinnamon and vanilla extract

- Apple peels, lemon peels and vanilla extract

ESSENTIAL OILS

Some people love using essential oils to scent their homes and swear that there are health benefits to be had from essential oils on top of just the mood boost that you get from a cozy scent. Essential oils can be used to make a DIY room spray by mixing a few drops with water and 1 teaspoon (4 g) of baking soda in an empty spray bottle or you can just stick a few drops on some cotton balls and hide them in a few areas around the house. My favorite essential oil trick is to place a few drops on your furnace filter to instantly circulate that fresh scent throughout the whole house. So efficient!

HOW TO
FINALLY GET
YOUR ACT
TOGETHER

and Get Organized
Once and For All
(But For Real This Time)

Of course you always vow to finally get organized at least once a year. And of course you start off pretty well, but things never seem to work out quite the way you want them to. Why is that? What's the deal with organizing that makes it seem almost impossible? There are definitely some secrets out there that professional organizers use that make all the difference *and* there are some tricks that really work for making things finally stick! Of course, I have them all lined up and waiting for you here, ready to be wrapped up and brought home! If you're all set to actually get this done, but for real this time, here's what you need to do.

MAKE AN INVESTMENT

If you want to get something out of this organizational process, then you're going to first have to put something into it. It has to be something valuable to you and something you're not just willing to throw away once you start feeling lazy a little way into your organizing journey. This might be time, it might be money or it might be both. For me, as soon as I started investing in a few organizational tools to help keep my things in order, I was really able to stick to the whole process *and* actually be really excited about the progress I was making. It was fun to have new pretty things that allowed me to enjoy all my stuff that I had organized, and I wasn't willing to let all of those dollars spent (not very many, mind you) go to waste. If you want to get your organizing done on a budget, you absolutely can still make a difference. This doesn't mean that you have to just line all your stuff up haphazardly in one corner of a room and be happy with it—it just means that you'll need to invest more time, rather than money, into the process. You can make DIY versions of almost any shelf, cabinet or storage bin with a few simple materials and a little cleverness.

DIY FABRIC-COVERED STORAGE BOX

ITEMS NEEDED:

- Box

- Fabric big enough to cover the box

- Scissors

- Glue stick

- Glue gun

- Wide ribbon for trimming edges

- Label windows (optional)

Iron your fabric and place your box in the center. Turn your box over onto one side and trace the outline. Return the box to the center of the fabric. Repeat this process on all four sides.

Cut out your fabric and apply the glue stick to the bottom of the box. Place the box down in the center of the fabric.

Apply the glue stick to the sides of the box and smooth the fabric up and over the inside lip. Repeat this process on all four sides.

Apply the ribbon trim to all four corners of the box using the glue gun, then apply the ribbon trim around the top lip of the box for a nice finished look.

Attach your label window and put your new storage bin to good use!

CREATE A HOME FOR EVERYTHING

You knew that, right? A place for everything and everything in its place. That saying just feels so old-fashioned to most people that it can't possibly have any place in today's modern home, but it's really the key to all things organizational. Or at least one of the keys. If you have a thing, an item, a pile of stuff that's hanging around without a real place where it's supposed to go when all's right in the world and everything's put away, then you need to figure that out. We get so used to having so many things without permanent places to live in our homes that we just sort of start to think that we have to be constantly on our toes when it comes to tidying up, coming up with temporary solutions that are somehow supposed to work decently over and over again. But that doesn't work decently at all, does it? So when you come across some things that aren't in their ideal, permanent home, take a moment. Realize that these things are out of place and consciously make a note to come up with a permanent solution, either by rearranging items, purchasing some new organizational supplies that will actually work for your problem, creating a brilliant storage solution of your own with your bare hands or some combination of all of those possibilities. And then, of course, do it.

BE REALISTIC (IF IT'S NOT WORKING, IT'S NOT WORKING)

This will make all the difference. All. The. Difference. There might be some storage solutions that you *think* should work just fine, but because of your current lifestyle or your family situation, they just don't. If you have toddlers in the house, for example. We renovated our en suite bathroom beautifully one year and put every storage solution known to man in the vanity. It was amazing. There truly was a place for everything. And we even had extra storage just outside the door so nothing would ever be cramped or overly full. Then I spent the next two years getting ready in the living room and keeping all of my toiletry items in there. Having the toddler in the en suite bathroom with me just never worked (as much as I wanted it to) and only created a giant mess for me to clean up later, so I got ready in the living room where he could play with his toys and the mess was easily contained. I found a nice old wooden toolbox at an antique store and used that to hold all of my toiletry items and it worked quite well. It took me awhile before I could actually get ready in my en suite on a regular basis, but at least I didn't pull my hair out every morning trying to make myself presentable.

TREAT EXTRA STORAGE SPACES LIKE GOLD

If you're lucky enough to have an extra space to use for storage, it could be all of your wildest organizational dreams coming true! Oftentimes, the very best storage spaces are the neglected rooms that really don't seem good for anything else, like the dark basement, the oddly shaped attic or that weird extra room that no one can really find a use for. We toss things in there willy-nilly and don't even think twice about it, because these rooms are usually just so unattractive for everyday use that we don't consider them salvageable in any way. In my one-hundred-year-old basement, we have low ceilings, a crumbling floor and all kinds of mechanical stuff out in the open. We used to toss all of our unwanted items down there, while trying to keep all of our extra well-loved items upstairs in the main living spaces where there just wasn't room for them. As soon as I realized what a great opportunity I had in the basement for storing seasonal items, decor stuff and even extra toys, my whole house started to feel cleaner and so much easier to keep organized. If you have a neglected space like this, invest in some good, basic shelving, a label maker and lots of easy-to-use storage bins. Start treating it like it's the storage room of your dreams, and pretty soon it will be!

GET RID OF STUFF

Sometimes you need to rearrange your storage areas to make room for the things that you love and that you want to store properly. And sometimes rearranging your items means moving them somewhere else entirely. Like, outside of your house. Like, off of your property. And out of your possession. Decluttering is absolutely at the very heart of the entire organizational process. A lot of people who have a goal of getting organized really just have too much stuff, but they always think that if they just worked a little harder, moved things around a little more and somehow were just a little cleverer, they would have room for everything. If this sounds like a familiar scenario, then you're not alone. But seriously, you need to stop doing this to yourself. You don't need all of this stuff. You don't even really like all of this stuff. And you're certainly not *using* all of this stuff. As a former hoarder of knickknacks, tchotchkes and other decor items that I could maybe use "someday," I have to tell you, life is so much better on the other side of the decluttering mountain. When you only have a few favorite items left on your overstuffed shelf, it's suddenly so easy to find somewhere for things to go. You'll even walk by that area and catch yourself thinking that you almost look like you know what you're doing when it comes to this organizing stuff. You know those "super organized" people who you always thought were so smart and were able to make their homes look like they just "have it all together"? The ones who you thought knew some kind of secret formula to make rooms magically look organized? Yup, you guessed right. The only magic there was the magic of decluttering. They may have learned it a little bit before you did, but now you're on to the trick, too! The key to success in decluttering is to go easy on yourself.

You don't need to find a suitably loving home for every cheap dollar-store item. And you don't need to sell everything to get back every possible penny of lost money. You don't. I'm absolving you of that guilt right now. In fact, a lot of what you're getting rid of really is just trash, so toss it all without restraint! For the few items that you really think should be donated, round them all up and bring them somewhere that can take everything at once, like one of the larger thrift stores with different departments. Just get rid of your junk and get rid of it fast. Again, this is all about making things easy on you. And what's easier than getting the almost instant reward of a clear, stress-free space? Honestly. Get rid of your excess, and everything else will start to fall into place almost immediately.

CHECKLIST:
WHAT TO DO
Each Day

Ideally, you'll eventually come up with your own perfect daily to-do list to keep things running smoothly and looking tidy in the quickest and easiest way possible, based on your own schedule and your home's needs. I should also add that, ideally, this list will change frequently to suit the changes and needs in your schedule for different seasons, activities and preferences. Sometimes, though, it's nice to have a jumping-off point to get you started, something that you can test out and then customize yourself. This list is just that: a basic daily to-do list of things that will go a long way to keeping your home clean and shiny without demanding a lot of your time.

☐ Make your beds

☐ Do *some* laundry

☐ Deal with your dishes

☐ Change any full or nearly full trash cans

☐ Do a quick bathroom wipe-down

☐ Wipe your kitchen counters and kitchen table

☐ Do a swift sweeping of your kitchen floor

☐ Spot-mop any spills or scuffs on hard floors

☐ Declutter and clear a few surfaces

CHECKLIST:
WHAT TO DO
Every Month

Here, we have some ideas for bigger jobs that you can add to your monthly to-do list. If you can complete each one of these quick, bite-size tasks each month, you'll be amazed at what a difference you'll see in your home!

ALL OVER THE HOME

☐ Seriously vacuum each room of the house (spot-vacuum on an as-needed basis throughout the rest of the month)

☐ Dust the tops of door and window frames and clear any cobwebs

☐ Spot-wipe the walls and trim in each room

☐ Wipe down your switch plates and doorknobs

☐ Check your main coat closet/rack and clear out anything out of season or unnecessary

☐ Check all your mirrors, windows and glass for fingerprints and smudges

☐ Clean your blinds and window coverings as needed

☐ Wipe down and polish any wooden tables, chairs and other furniture

☐ Spot-clean your upholstery and carpets

☐ Declutter any extra magazines and catalogs that you've already read

☐ Switch out your seasonal decor or make a few changes that make your space feel freshened up

☐ Wipe down your indoor and outdoor light fixtures; remove any glass parts (if possible) and polish them

IN THE KITCHEN AND FOOD STORAGE AREAS

- ❑ Empty and clean your fridges and freezers; replace everything and reorganize
- ❑ Clean your stove and oven if needed
- ❑ Clean your vent hood filters
- ❑ Clean your microwave and wipe down your other small appliances
- ❑ Wipe down your cabinets
- ❑ Tidy and clean the under-sink area
- ❑ Wipe down your trash can
- ❑ Check all your drawers and cupboards to see if they need reorganizing

IN THE BATHROOMS

- ❑ Wash all of your rugs and bath mats
- ❑ Wash your shower curtains and liners
- ❑ Clean all your toothbrush holders, soap dispensers and other accessories
- ❑ Throw away any empty or expired bottles
- ❑ Wash your kids' bath toys
- ❑ Descale your faucets and showerheads as needed

IN THE BEDROOMS

- ☐ Wash all the mattress pads, bed skirts and pillow covers

- ☐ Vacuum under the bed

- ☐ Clear off and declutter your bedside tables, dressers and shelves

- ☐ Remove any damaged, ill-fitting or outdated clothes from your closets and drawers to donate or throw away

- ☐ Check all your dresser drawers for organization and refold clothes where necessary

- ☐ Straighten all the hangers and shelves in your closets

- ☐ Straighten your shoes

- ☐ Dust all the closet shelves and hanging rods

IN THE HOME OFFICE

- ☐ Clean your various screens and keyboards

- ☐ Organize writing utensils

- ☐ Throw out any trash or old paperwork

- ☐ Restock the printer paper and ink

- ☐ Remove any unnecessary papers from files

Just one or two of these jobs a day should do the trick! You may notice that a lot of the things that you might normally do on a more regular basis have been left off of both the daily and monthly cleaning checklists, like watering plants or changing the sheets on your beds. When you're using your ninja cleaning skills, you'll be able to identify and tackle these jobs on an ongoing, as-needed basis, and you won't need to worry about working them into an over-complicated, ongoing cleaning schedule. The tasks in these monthly cleaning lists are some ideas for things you'll want to add into your mini ninja cleaning lists about once every month for a house that feels like it's had a nice monthly deep clean—without actually having to do a huge deep clean every single month!

CHECKLIST:
SUPER-MEGA
ALL-INCLUSIVE
Deep-Cleaning

Sometimes you want it all. Maybe you just really love cleaning. Maybe you want a complete fresh start to kick off your newfound love of quickly keeping a clean home. This is the list that has absolutely everything covered for those times when you really want to go all out. Breathe deeply before you dive into this list and remember to use it with caution. Or with reckless abandon for the love of a clean house. Whichever suits you best!

ENTRYWAY AREAS

☐ Dust the ceilings and tops of door frames, window frames and doors

☐ Wipe down any doors, door frames, window frames and trim

☐ Wipe any marks off the walls

☐ Polish any windows or glass doors

☐ Clean all the light fixtures

☐ Wipe down any doorknobs and switch plates

☐ Sweep or vacuum the floors, including under furniture

☐ Clean any window coverings or blinds

☐ Sweep your front porch, landing, deck and/or stairs

☐ Clean any doormats or rugs, either in the washing machine or with the garden hose, and replace as needed

☐ Repot any plants that need it

☐ Wipe down planters

☐ Shake out and vacuum wreaths and other decorations

☐ Wipe down any benches, chairs, cabinets or other furniture pieces

☐ Declutter the coat closet or rack and straighten hangers, shelves and cubbies

LIVING ROOM, FAMILY ROOM, REC ROOM AND DEN

❐ Dust the ceilings and tops of door frames, window frames and doors

❐ Wipe down any doors, door frames, window frames and trim

❐ Wipe any marks off the walls

❐ Polish any windows or glass doors

❐ Clean all the light fixtures and lamps

❐ Wipe down any doorknobs and switch plates

❐ Sweep or vacuum the floors, including under furniture

❐ Shampoo carpets and rugs

❐ Vacuum all upholstered furniture and clean it according to the manufacturer's instructions

❐ Polish any wood furniture

❐ Clean any window coverings or blinds

❐ Remove everything from shelves and cabinets and dust thoroughly inside and out

❐ Wipe down all decorative items or place them in the dishwasher if it's appropriate

❐ Remove cushion covers and wash them, then iron them before putting them back

❐ Empty out any baskets or bins, vacuum them out and wipe them clean (or use wood polish)

❐ Clean remotes and other electronics carefully with rubbing alcohol

❐ Clean all mirrors and glass picture frame fronts

❐ Clean out any end table or coffee table drawers

- ☐ Clean out your fireplace
- ☐ Water any plants and wipe each leaf gently to remove dust
- ☐ Clean any fake plants
- ☐ Clear out magazine and catalog racks

PLAYROOM

- ☐ Dust the ceilings and tops of door frames, window frames and doors
- ☐ Wipe down any doors, door frames, window frames and trim
- ☐ Wipe any marks off the walls
- ☐ Polish any windows or glass doors
- ☐ Clean all the light fixtures and lamps
- ☐ Wipe down any doorknobs and switch plates
- ☐ Sweep or vacuum the floors, including under furniture
- ☐ Shampoo carpets and rugs
- ☐ Vacuum all upholstered furniture and clean it according to the manufacturer's instructions
- ☐ Clean any window coverings or blinds
- ☐ Reorganize toys and return everything to its proper home
- ☐ Inspect toys for wear and tear and discard any that can't be repaired
- ☐ Remove a few toys that are no longer used and donate them (ask your kids for help with this one, so you know which ones they're ready to get rid of if they're old enough)
- ☐ Wipe down large toys
- ☐ Spot-clean soft toys

- ☐ Wash small plastic toys in the dishwasher
- ☐ Add new bins, baskets or shelving units if they're needed
- ☐ Dust shelving units
- ☐ Vacuum, dust and wipe down any bins or baskets
- ☐ Organize bookshelves and repair any damaged books

DINING ROOM

- ☐ Dust the ceilings and tops of door frames, window frames and doors
- ☐ Wipe down any doors, door frames, window frames and trim
- ☐ Wipe any marks off the walls
- ☐ Polish any windows or glass doors
- ☐ Clean all the light fixtures and lamps
- ☐ Wipe down any doorknobs and switch plates
- ☐ Sweep or vacuum the floors, including under furniture
- ☐ Shampoo carpets and rugs
- ☐ Vacuum all upholstered furniture and clean it according to the manufacturer's instructions
- ☐ Clean any window coverings or blinds
- ☐ Carefully dust shelving units and china cabinets inside and out
- ☐ Wash dishes, crystal, drinkware and servingware and put them away
- ☐ Polish silver
- ☐ Make sure all stored table linens are clean and ironed

- ☐ Polish any wooden furniture, including table and chair legs
- ☐ Water any plants and wipe down each leaf
- ☐ Clean any fake plants
- ☐ Clean all mirrors and glass picture frame fronts
- ☐ Wipe down any other decorative items or put them in the dishwasher if it's appropriate

KITCHEN

- ☐ Dust the ceilings and tops of door frames, window frames and doors
- ☐ Wipe down any doors, door frames, window frames and trim
- ☐ Wipe any marks off the walls
- ☐ Polish any windows or glass doors
- ☐ Clean all the light fixtures
- ☐ Wipe down any doorknobs and switch plates
- ☐ Sweep or vacuum the floors, including under furniture
- ☐ Remove and clean all the window coverings and blinds
- ☐ Clean your pet dishes and surrounding areas
- ☐ Clean and organize under your sink
- ☐ Wipe down all the cabinets
- ☐ Remove everything from the counters and wipe them down
- ☐ Empty and wash all your countertop canisters and trays
- ☐ Reseal any stone counters, floors and backsplashes

- [ ] Wipe down all your small appliances
- [ ] Wipe down the tile backsplash and scrub and reseal the grout as needed
- [ ] Wipe down the vent hood and clean the filters
- [ ] Empty each drawer and cupboard, wipe it down, then declutter and reorganize it
- [ ] Empty the refrigerator and freezer and wipe them down, then declutter and reorganize them
- [ ] Clean your dishwasher inside and out and run a maintenance/cleaning cycle
- [ ] Clean your stove and oven
- [ ] Clean your microwave inside and out
- [ ] Wash any decorative items on your counters, tables and walls

BATHROOMS

- [ ] Dust the ceilings and tops of door frames, window frames and doors
- [ ] Wipe down any doors, door frames, window frames and trim
- [ ] Wipe any marks off the walls
- [ ] Polish any windows or glass doors
- [ ] Clean all the light fixtures
- [ ] Wipe down any doorknobs and switch plates
- [ ] Sweep or vacuum the floors, including under furniture

- ☐ Clean rugs and bath mats
- ☐ Clean shower curtains and liners
- ☐ Remove and clean the window coverings and blinds
- ☐ Remove your vent fan cover and vacuum inside
- ☐ Descale the faucets and showerheads
- ☐ Scrub your tub, shower, sink and toilet
- ☐ Clean the shower glass and apply water-spot prevention if desired
- ☐ Empty all the shelves and cabinets, wipe them down and reorganize them
- ☐ Remove any bottles of products that are expired or that you don't use
- ☐ Wipe down all your cabinet door fronts
- ☐ Remove everything from your counters and wipe them down
- ☐ Empty and wash all of your countertop canisters and trays
- ☐ Reseal any stone counters, floors and backsplashes
- ☐ Wipe down all of your electric hair styling tools
- ☐ Clean your hairbrushes
- ☐ Clean your makeup brushes
- ☐ Refold all of your towels and washcloths and rewash them to freshen if needed
- ☐ Make a list of any items that need restocking, like soap, shampoo, toothpaste, toilet paper or cotton balls
- ☐ Wash any decorative items

LAUNDRY ROOM

☐ Dust the ceilings and tops of door frames, window frames and doors

☐ Wipe down any doors, door frames, window frames and trim

☐ Wipe any marks off the walls

☐ Polish any windows or glass doors

☐ Clean all the light fixtures

☐ Wipe down any doorknobs and switch plates

☐ Sweep or vacuum the floors, including under furniture and appliances

☐ Clean any window coverings or blinds

☐ Clean your dryer exhaust vent inside and where it vents outside of your house

☐ Clean your dryer lint trap with a long brush and your vacuum cleaner

☐ Wipe down both of your machines inside and out and run a cleaning cycle in your washing machine

☐ Empty any cupboards or shelves and wipe them down

☐ Declutter any empty bottles or laundry products that you don't use and reorganize the ones you're keeping

☐ Make a list of any laundry items that need to be restocked

MASTER BEDROOM

☐ Dust the ceilings and tops of door frames, window frames and doors

☐ Wipe down any doors, door frames, window frames and trim

☐ Wipe any marks off the walls

- ☐ Polish any windows or glass doors
- ☐ Clean all the light fixtures and lamps
- ☐ Wipe down any doorknobs and switch plates
- ☐ Sweep or vacuum the floors, including under furniture
- ☐ Shampoo carpets and rugs
- ☐ Vacuum all upholstered furniture and clean it according to the manufacturer's instructions
- ☐ Polish any wood furniture
- ☐ Clean any window coverings or blinds
- ☐ Wash your mattress pad, pillow covers and bed skirt
- ☐ Vacuum your mattress, flip it, then vacuum it again
- ☐ Clear off all bedside tables, desks and dressers, declutter them and wipe them down
- ☐ Dust and tidy any bookshelves
- ☐ Remove any damaged, ill-fitting or outdated clothes from your closets and drawers to donate or throw away
- ☐ Check all your dresser drawers for organization and refold clothes where necessary
- ☐ Straighten all the hangers and shelves in your closets
- ☐ Straighten your shoes
- ☐ Dust all the closet shelves and hanging rods
- ☐ Wipe down all your decorative items on horizontal surfaces and walls
- ☐ Water any plants and wipe off each leaf
- ☐ Shake out and clean any fake plants
- ☐ Dust and polish any electronics

KIDS' ROOMS

- ☐ Dust the ceilings and tops of door frames, window frames and doors
- ☐ Wipe down any doors, door frames, window frames and trim
- ☐ Wipe any marks off the walls
- ☐ Polish any windows or glass doors
- ☐ Clean all the light fixtures and lamps
- ☐ Wipe down any doorknobs and switch plates
- ☐ Sweep or vacuum the floors, including under furniture
- ☐ Shampoo carpets and rugs
- ☐ Vacuum all upholstered furniture and clean it according to the manufacturer's instructions
- ☐ Polish any wood furniture
- ☐ Clean any window coverings or blinds
- ☐ Check the drawers and closet for clothes that have been outgrown and set them aside for donation or hand-me-downs
- ☐ Refold the clothes in any messy drawers and straighten the closet
- ☐ Take all toys out of any bins or baskets or off of shelves and wipe them down
- ☐ Declutter any unused toys and reorganize the ones that you're keeping
- ☐ Straighten any other games and books
- ☐ Wash the mattress pad, pillow covers and bed skirt
- ☐ Vacuum the mattress, flip it, then vacuum it again
- ☐ Clear off all bedside tables, desks and dressers, declutter them and wipe them down
- ☐ Wipe down any decorative items on the horizontal surfaces or the walls
- ☐ Dust and polish any electronics

SPARE BEDROOMS

☐ Dust the ceilings and tops of door frames, window frames and doors

☐ Wipe down any doors, door frames, window frames and trim

☐ Wipe any marks off the walls

☐ Polish any windows or glass doors

☐ Clean all the light fixtures and lamps

☐ Wipe down any doorknobs and switch plates

☐ Sweep or vacuum the floors, including under furniture

☐ Shampoo carpets and rugs

☐ Vacuum all upholstered furniture and clean it according to the manufacturer's instructions

☐ Polish any wood furniture

☐ Clean any window coverings or blinds

☐ Wash the mattress pad, pillow covers and bed skirt

☐ Vacuum the mattress, flip it, then vacuum it again

☐ Clear off all bedside tables, desks and dressers, declutter them and wipe them down

☐ Wipe down any decorative items on the horizontal surfaces or the walls

☐ Dust and reorganize any computer, craft and sewing areas if they're in that room

☐ Dust and polish any electronics

HOME OFFICE

☐ Dust the ceilings and tops of door frames, window frames and doors

☐ Wipe down any doors, door frames, window frames and trim

☐ Wipe any marks off the walls

☐ Polish any windows or glass doors

☐ Clean all the light fixtures and lamps

☐ Wipe down any doorknobs and switch plates

☐ Sweep or vacuum the floors, including under furniture

☐ Shampoo carpets and rugs

☐ Vacuum all upholstered furniture and clean it according to the manufacturer's instructions

☐ Polish any wood furniture

☐ Clean any window coverings or blinds

☐ Clean your various screens, keyboards and other equipment

☐ Organize the writing utensils

☐ Throw out any trash or old paperwork

☐ Restock the printer paper and ink

☐ Remove any unnecessary papers from files

☐ Clear off your desk and wipe it down

☐ Clear out unnecessary computer files, downloads and bookmarks

☐ Organize digital pictures by year and event

CRAFT ROOM, HOBBY ROOM OR WORKSHOP

- ☐ Dust the ceilings and tops of door frames, window frames and doors
- ☐ Wipe down any doors, door frames, window frames and trim
- ☐ Wipe any marks off the walls
- ☐ Polish any windows or glass doors
- ☐ Clean all the light fixtures and lamps
- ☐ Wipe down any doorknobs and switch plates
- ☐ Sweep or vacuum the floors, including under furniture
- ☐ Clean any window coverings or blinds
- ☐ Go through each storage area and remove anything that is empty or broken or that doesn't get used
- ☐ Clear all of your desks, tables and workspaces and wipe them down
- ☐ Put everything back in an organized way that maximizes the amount of open horizontal space that you have for working
- ☐ Inspect your storage solutions and consider whether you need to add anything

OTHER STORAGE AREAS

❏ Dust the ceilings and tops of door frames, window frames and doors

❏ Wipe down any doors, door frames, window frames and trim

❏ Wipe any marks off the walls

❏ Polish any windows or glass doors

❏ Clean all the light fixtures and lamps

❏ Wipe down any doorknobs and switch plates

❏ Sweep or vacuum the floors, including under furniture

❏ Clean any window coverings or blinds

❏ Organize your linen closet, refold and tidy linens and add baskets where needed; rewash items as needed

❏ Remove any outdated or unused food or food prep items from your pantry, wipe down your shelves, straighten all your stored items and inspect your storage solutions to see if you need to add anything to help the room function better

❏ Open each seasonal decor bin and review all the contents; remove and donate or discard anything that you haven't used in years or that you don't absolutely love

❏ Open all your other storage bins, one by one, and review items such as old clothes, kids' school papers and old electronics; donate or discard anything that is outdated, hasn't been used in years, probably won't be used for years or that doesn't bring back fond memories

❏ Wipe down all your shelving and plastic storage bins

PET AREAS

☐ Dust the ceilings and tops of door frames, window frames and doors

☐ Wipe down any doors, door frames, window frames and trim

☐ Wipe any marks off the walls

☐ Polish any windows or glass doors

☐ Clean all the light fixtures and lamps

☐ Wipe down any doorknobs and switch plates

☐ Sweep or vacuum the floors, including under furniture

☐ Clean any window coverings or blinds

☐ Clean the food and water dishes

☐ Empty out any litter boxes, spray them down with the hose and leave them to dry thoroughly in the sun if it's possible

☐ Refill litter boxes with fresh litter and top it with baking soda

☐ Clean any food scoops or storage canisters in the dishwasher

☐ Clean pet brushes

☐ Clean pet beds

☐ Organize storage for brushes, shampoos and medications

☐ Organize collars and leashes

☐ Inspect everything and make a list of anything that needs replacing or that you need more of

GARAGE/UTILITY AREAS

☐ Dust the ceilings and tops of door frames, window frames and doors

☐ Wipe down any doors, door frames, window frames and trim

☐ Wipe any marks off the walls

☐ Polish any windows or glass doors

☐ Clean all the light fixtures and lamps

☐ Wipe down any doorknobs and switch plates

☐ Sweep the floor

☐ Replace furnace and A/C vents

☐ Wipe down the dehumidifier inside and out

☐ Wipe down the hot water tank and furnace

☐ Check for good airflow around the A/C unit and clear away any brush or weeds as needed

☐ Wipe down your brooms, mops, buckets and vacuum cleaner; remove any tangled hairs or fibers from your vacuum cleaner carpet attachment with small scissors or a stitch ripper

OUTDOORS

- ☐ Power wash your house's exterior siding, patios, decks and outdoor furniture
- ☐ Wash the outsides of all your windows
- ☐ Move all your plant pots and wash underneath them
- ☐ Wipe down the outsides of your plant pots
- ☐ Shake out your wreaths and vacuum them
- ☐ Wipe down mailboxes, house numbers and outdoor light fixtures
- ☐ Sweep your porch or landing and shake out the mat
- ☐ Clear your gutters and downspouts
- ☐ Inspect the weather stripping on your doors and replace as needed
- ☐ Clean your outdoor grill inside and out and inspect the cover to make sure it's still in good shape
- ☐ Wipe down any outdoor pillows, cushions and umbrellas to remove dust and pollen buildup
- ☐ Add new mulch to your flowerbeds
- ☐ Empty garbage and recycling bins and spray them with the hose or power washer then leave them in the sun to dry
- ☐ Wash and sharpen your garden tools and apply oil to prevent rust
- ☐ Spray down any outdoor toys and leave them to dry in the sun
- ☐ Inspect your outdoor storage solutions for toys, garden tools and so on and decide if you need to add anything

ACKNOWLEDGMENTS

Thank you...

To Grammy, for watching the kids for me so I could get "just a little bit of work done," yet again. To the kids, for sharing their time with me with this book and all of my silly cleaning experiments. To Sarah, for the never-ending stream of encouragement and exclamation marks (!!!!!). To all of my parents, who taught me what it means to have a beautiful, happy, reasonably clean home. To Chris, for always answering my ideas for big, crazy projects like this one with "Do it!"

ABOUT THE AUTHOR

 *Courtenay Hartford* writes about her Southwestern Ontario, Canada farmhouse on the blog The Creek Line House. As an avid DIYer and homekeeping enthusiast, she enjoys showing her readers clever tips for making life around the house seem easy-peasy as well as fun renovation and decorating projects. As a busy wife, mom of 2 and pet-parent of 3, Courtenay understands all of the challenges of a hectic family life and is passionate about helping people "work smarter, not harder" in their homes, whether that means learning to keep up with the constant mess that comes along with the toddler lifestyle, or finally getting the nerve to tackle that DIY project that will truly make a house feel like a home.

INDEX